I0129022

Pellegrino Antonio Orlandi, James Marks

The History and Art of Engraving

Pellegrino Antonio Orlandi, James Marks

The History and Art of Engraving

ISBN/EAN: 9783744648868

Printed in Europe, USA, Canada, Australia, Japan

Cover: Foto ©Suzi / pixelio.de

More available books at **www.hansebooks.com**

Sculptura Historico-Technica :

OR, THE

HISTORY AND ART

OF

ENGRAVING.

CONTAINING,

I. The Rife and Progrefs of ENGRAVING.

II. Of ENGRAVING in general.

III. Of ENGRAVING, ETCHING, and SCRAPING on COPPER, as now practifed.

IV. An Idea of a Fine Collection of PRINTS.

V. The REPERTORIUM; or, A COLLECTION of various MARKS and CYPHERS, with Additions.

To which is now added,

A Chronological and Hiftorical Series of the PAINTERS from the Eleventh Century.

Extracted from

BALDINUCCI, FLORENT LE COMPTE, FAIRTHORNE, the ABECEDARIO PITTORICO, and other Authors.

With COPPER-PLATES.

The FOURTH EDITION.

LONDON:

Printed for J. MARKS, in *St. Martin's Lane.*
M DCC LXX.

THE

PREFACE.

TO render a Treatife on any Art or Science acceptable to every Reader, it fhould certainly be calculated to inftruct as well as entertain; and in order to fulfil this Intention, it is neceffary that Ideas fhould be prefented to us in fuch a Manner, as to make a ftrong and lafting Impreffion upon our Minds: I flatter myfelf that proper Attention has been paid to both thefe Circumftances in the following Treatife, which has hitherto been received as an ufeful as well as an agreeable Work.

Every

Every curious Enquirer muſt receive infinite Satisfaction, in tracing the various Improvements of any of the Arts from their primary Sources, and obſerving with Care the Difficulties they encounter in their Progreſs towards Perfection: But, his Labour will be conſiderably diminiſhed, if he ſhould be aſſiſted in the Proſecution of his Enquiries by the Induſtry and Attention of others who have before treated on the Subject; for by this Means much Light will be thrown upon the Point in Queſtion, and he will be prevented from falling into thoſe Errors which he probably would not have eſcaped, had he been left to his own Conjectures.

The Antients are generally allowed to have excelled in the Art of Painting; though very few of their Works have been handed down to us, as it was impoſſible

poffible to preferve them from the In-
juries of Time and other Accidents :
Engraving however, ftepped in with
its Affiftance, and eftablifhed a lafting
Memorial of its Ufefulnefs, by the Pre-
fervation of many beautiful Pieces in
Painting, as well as in Sculpture, Architecture &c. the Originals of which
have been deftroyed : Painters and other
Artifts therefore, are as much obliged to
the Invention as the Public; for without it, many of their moft capital.
and valuable Performances would have
been loft. It may indeed be objected,
that Defigning could have anfwered
thefe Purpofes; but let it be confidered,
that Drawings as well as Paintings are
generally confined to a few Poffeffors;
whereas by the Art of Engraving, a
Number of Impreffions may be taken
from one Plate, without the leaft Devi-
ation of a fingle Line.

A 3

The

The Reader will be led from the Rife of this Art through its various Stages to that Degree of Perfection which it has acquired in the prefent Age: The Hiftorical Part comes firft; Secondly, the Art in general; Thirdly, Etching; Fourthly, Metzotinto; and Fifthly, an Idea of a fine Collection of Prints; which part deferves particular attention, as the Gentleman will here have proper Rules to affift him in the choice and difpofition of his Collection, which, when properly arranged, will afford him a Fund of rational Amufement for his leifure Hours. Sixthly, the Characters, or Marks and Cyphers ufed by Engravers &c. with their explanation; Seventhly, the Initials ufed by fome Artifts inftead of Marks or Cyphers, or by the fame at other Times; Eighthly, will be given a Chronological and Hiftorical Series of Painters from

the

the eleventh Century to the prefent Time; Ninthly, the Student will be furnifhed with an Alphabetical Index of the Chriftian and Surnames &c. and laftly, with an Alphabetical Lift of the Surnames before the Chriftian Names.

This Edition is rendered more complete by the infertion of feveral Marks omitted in the former, together with the Chronological Series; the whole being difpofed in a regular Manner, the feveral Parts following each other as the Subject leads, which Method I hope will be moft agreeable to the Reader.

T H E

THE

CONTENTS.

Page

The

The CONTENTS.

THE

THE

HISTORY,

OF THE

ART *of* ENGRAVING.

O F all the Arts which are defcended from *Defigning*, none, except Architecture, Painting, and Sculpture, has given fo much Pleafure, or has been of more Ufe, to all Lovers and Profeffors of the Liberal Sciences, than that of *Engraving* ; whether on Copper, or Wood : for, by this Means, all the celebrated Performances and Inventions of the moft eminent Mafters, are exceedingly well imitated, and reduced to fo fmall a Size, as to be communicable to the whole World. 'Tis by the Affiftance of this Art, thofe who have never croffed the Seas, are acquainted with the magnificent Structures, beautiful Statues, inimitable Paintings, *&c.* with which the Cities, Churches and Palaces of other Countries, and particularly *Italy*, are adorned : Which is a fingular Pleafure to the Lovers of thofe Arts, and of no lefs Ufe to thofe who

B   profefs

profefs them; for, as it is an eviden
Truth, that we have no Ideas but wha
arife from Senfation, fo confequently th
readieft Way to form them, is by con
templating the noble Works of others.

This Art, which by the beft Authors i
placed among the μονοχρωμαΐοι, was acci
dentally difcovered in the fourteenth Cen
tury, by one *Mafo Finiguerra*, an inge
nious Goldfmith and Sculptor of *Florence*
who was famous not only for defigning
and emboffing Figures on Gold and othe
Metals, but alfo for engraving, and after
wards inlaying them with Metals of othe.
Colours; which he did in the following
Manner. Having defigned and engravec
his Figures, he ufed, before he inlayec
them, to fill the Engraving with Earth
and caft melted Sulphur on it, which gavi
it a Sort of an Olive Colour; after which
preffing a Piece of damp Paper on it
with a fmooth wooden Roller, the En
graving on the Metal remained imprintec
on the Paper, juft as if it had been de
figned with a Pen. *Baccio Baldini*, ano
ther Gold and Silver-Smith of the fami
City, began to do the fame; but as h
underftood very little of Defigning him
felf, he employed *Sandro Botticelli* to affif
him in moft of his Performances: Somi
of which being feen by *Antonio del Pol*
laiolo

laiolo, a celebrated Defigner of the fame City alfo, who had ftudied Anatomy to learn the Situation and Action of the Muf- cles of the human Body; he engraved fome of his own Defigns on Copper, and amongft the reft a fine Keprefentation of a Battle.

This new Manner of Defigning began now to be the Subject of Converfation, and *Andrew Mantegna*, who was then at *Rome*, having feen fome of thefe Prints, was fo exceedingly pleafed with them, that he ap- plied himfelf with the greateft Diligence to engraving his Triumphs; which being pro- bably the firft Prints that appeared in Pub- lick, met with univerfal Applaufe, and ob- tained him great Part of that Glory, which was due to the firft Inventors of this Art, becaufe he, by great Study and Applica- tion, brought it to a tolerable Degree of Perfection. But if *Mantegna*, after what he did, had boafted that he had perfected this Art; his Vanity would have deferved as juftly to be laughed at, as old *Palæmon*'s Tears, who lamented bitterly, believing the World by his Death would lofe the Ufe of Letters: For whoever rightly con- fiders, will fee very clearly, that this fine Art of *Engraving*, firft with the *Graver*, and afterwards with *Aqua Fortis*, in the Courfe of about 280 Years, fince *Man- tegna*'s Death, has made fuch Progrefs,

B 2   and

and is arrived at fuch Perfection, that it is
not only, as I have faid, of great Ufe to
the Profeffors of Architecture, Painting,
Sculpture, &c. by communicating to them
the noble Inventions of others; but to all
Mankind in general, by acquainting them
with whatever is worthy of Obfervation,
even in the moft diftant Parts of the Globe.
However, we muft do this Juftice to *Mantegna's* Memory, to acknowledge, that
what he did, excited others, after his Example, to apply themfelves to this Art;
fince in 1490, *Germany* produced *Il Tedefco*, and *Ifrael Martin*, who firft fhewed
an uncommon Diligence in their Works,
and gave this Art to the renowned *Albert
Durer*, their Difciple, *Lucas* of *Leyden*,
Aldegrave, and others, who afterwards became much abler Artifts than their Mafters.
And indeed, to fay the Truth, from this
Time, the *Graver* would have begun to
rival the Pencil, had not their Prints, imitating the *Drynefs* of the Paintings of thofe
Countries, which want much of the *Mel-
lownefs* and *Delicacy* of the *Italian*, been
lefs beautiful than they would otherwife
have been; which was not a little aug-
mented by the Variety of Invention, different Air of the Heads, and particular
new Manner of cloathing Figures, introduced into the Art of Painting by the eminent

nent *Italian* Masters, among which are reckoned *Bacchiacca,* *James* of *Pantormo,* and lastly, *Andrew del Sarto,* all *Florentines,* who were continually adding something new and graceful to their Works.

In the fifteenth Century, and Time of *Raphael,* *Italy* produced the celebrated *Mark Antonio Raimondi,* to whom this Art is very much indebted, as he was the first who began to reduce it to so fine a Manner, that even *Raphael* himself was so much pleased with it, as to desire him not only to engrave many of his best Paintings, but also a great Number of his Designs and fine Inventions, which 'till then had never been seen in *Rome,* or elsewhere. His Disciples and Imitators were *Augustin* of *Venice, Sylvester* and *Mark* of *Ravenna,* who, between the Years 1535 and 1560, engraved almost all *Raphael*'s Paintings, Designs, and Inventions; as also those of *Julio Romano,* his favourite Disciple, from his and *Raphael*'s own Designs. We have of *Augustin*'s Engraving, the fine Print of Anatomy, the Slaughter of the Innocents, and naked Men, who are tormenting the Martyr Saint *Laurence* with Fire; all done from the beautiful Designs of *Baccio Bandinelli,* a famous Sculptor of *Florence:* The last Piece of which had the Reputation of exceeding the original Design.

fign. *John James Coraglio,* of *Verona,* alfo
imitated *Raimondi,* and engraved moft of
Roffo's Works, with many Defigns of *Perin del Vaga, Parmigianino,* and *Titian.*
After thefe, *Lamberto Suave* applied himfelf diligently to engraving, as may be feen
by his thirteen Prints of our bleffed Saviour,
and his twelve Apoftles; the fine Piece of
Saint *Paul* fitting and writing, and the
Story of the Refurrection of *Lazarus.*
John Baptifta, of *Mantua,* a Difciple of
Julio Romano, befides many Prints of Portraits, with a Sort of antique Crefts, publifhed two fine Pieces of the Burning of
Troy. There was alfo *Æneas Vico,* of
Parma, who engraved the Works and Defigns of *Roffo, Bandinelli,* and *Salviati,*
with many Books of ancient Medals, reprefenting the Effigies of the Emperors, and
their Wives, with their Reverfes; and alfo
the Genealogical Tables of the Emperors,
and of the Family of *Efte.* *Julio Bonafone*
engraved the Inventions of *Raphael, Julio
Romano, Parmigianino,* and others; and
Baptifta Franco publifhed many Prints of
other Mafters; and *Girolamo Cock,* a *Fleming,* engraved the fine Works of *Martin
Hemskirk,* his own Inventions, and thofe
of many other Mafters, which it would be
tedious to mention.

And

And as it is the particular Property of the human Underſtanding to be always in-venting ſomething, and as every Body has an innate Deſire to ſurpaſs the reſt of Man-kind by ſome peculiar Excellency; it was not long before *Hugo* of *Carpi*, a Painter of no great Renown in other Reſpects, be-gan to publiſh wooden Plates of two diffe-rent Impreſſions; the firſt of which ſhew-ed the *Shade*, juſt as Copper Plates do; and the ſecond, the *Light*; for the Wood being cut away very deep, left the *White* of the Paper, wherever there was Occaſion of Light; ſo that the Prints appeared as if they had been illuminated with *Spaniſh* White. He afterwards invented another Manner of Engraving, by which he made his Prints of three Impreſſions; that is to ſay, of the *deepeſt Shade*, the *lighteſt*, and of a *middling* one, making the *Lights* ap-pear in the White of the Leaf. He en-graved many of *Raphael*'s Works after this Manner, and was the Occaſion, that *Bal-thazar Peruzzi*, *Francis Parmigiano*, *An-thony* of *Trent*, *John Nicholas* of *Vicenza*, and *Dominico Beccafumi*, afterwards engra-ved many more of them in the ſame Man-ner, which ſucceeded ſo well, as to pleaſe the Lovers of this fine Art very much, and alſo be of great Uſe to them; but thoſe

B 4   moſt

moſt of all, that came from the Hand of *Beccaſumi.*

Cornelius Cort, a *Fleming,* ſucceeded theſe, and engraved the Landſkips, and other fine Works of *Girolamo Mutiano, Frederick* and *Taddeo Zucchero, Frederick Barrocio, Marcellus Venuſto of Mantua, Caravaggio,* and the inimitable Picture of the Transfiguration, by *Raphael.* There was alſo *Anthony Tempeſta,* who etched many Pieces of Battles, Huntings, and all Sorts of Animals, as I ſhall obſerve in his Life ; *Martin Rota,* who engraved the celebrated laſt Judgment of *Michael Angelo,* in two Plates, one of a greater, and the other of a leſſer Size, and ſeveral others from the Works of *Raphael* and *Frederico ; Cherubino Alberti,* who did many of *Polidoro's* Inventions ; and the never enough to be commended *Auguſtin Caracci,* whoſe moſt beautiful Prints are ſo well known to the Lovers of this Art, who were all eminent Maſters. *Villamena* of *Aſſiſi,* alſo a free, eaſy Engraver, and good Deſigner, publiſhed his Labours, amongſt which, the fine Print, of the Preſentation of our Saviour in the Temple, from the famous Picture of *Paul Veroneſe,* is very much eſteemed. In the Time of the Emperor *Rodolph, John* and *Raphael Sadalaer,* flouriſhed in

Germany,

Germany, and gave great Proofs of their Abilities by the many fine Plates which they published of the Works and Inventions of *Martin de Vos, Baſſan, Titian, Joſeph* of *Arpino*, and other Maſters. Their School produced *Egidius Sadalaer*, their Nephew, who was univerſally allowed to be the beſt Engraver of his Age, and led the Way to that fine Manner, which was copied by the beſt Maſters of the ſucceeding one. There was alſo *Raphael Guidi*, a *Tuſcan*, who engraved many fine Plates from the Works of *Joſeph* of *Arpino*; *Harman Muler*, a very bold and free Engraver; and the ingenious *Henry Goltius*, a *Hollander*, who had the Talent of imitating the Stile of many preceding Maſters; *Philip Tomaſini*, who engraved at *Rome* the Fall of *Lucifer*, the laſt Judgment, the Diſpute of our Saviour with the Doctors in the Temple, and the School of *Athens*, by *Raphael*, with many Inventions of other Maſters; *Matthew Greuter*, a Native of *Straſburg*, who, beſides engraving many Plates of his own Invention, retouched ſome of *Tempeſta*'s Plates of Hunting Pieces, and ſome of other Engravers; and *Theodore Crager*, whoſe fine Plate of the laſt Supper, from a famous Painting in *Freſco*, by *Andrew del Sarto*, is preſerved in the Grand Duke of

Tuſcany's

Tuscany's Wardrobe. We cannot behold
without Aftonifhment, the beautiful Prints
of *Saenredam*, and of the celebrated *Swan-burg*, who engraved the Defigns of *Rubens*
and *Bloemaert*, with extraordinary Delicacy.
The next, who became eminent, were
James Callot, who, for fmall Figures, excelled all his Predeceffors in this Art; and
the renowned *Stephen della Bella*, a *Floren-tine*. *Peter Tempefta*, a good Painter, etched about the fame Time his fine Inven-
tions; and *Salvator Rofa*, a *Neapolitan*, and
celebrated Landfkip Painter, publifhed
many of his comical Conceits; in which
the Trees and Herbage are touched with
furprizing Freedom; and after him, that
excellent Painter, and worthy Prieft, *Peter
Aquila*, who etched the admirable antique
Statues, and beautiful Paintings of *Hanni-bal Caracci*, in the Gallery of the *Farnefe*
Palace; and alfo the fine Works of *Lan-franco* in the *Villa Borghefe*; thofe of *Peter*
of *Cortona*, in the *Sachetti* Palace; and
fome of *Ciro Ferri*'s; with the noble Inventions of *Carlo Maratti*, and fome of his
own.

Some time after this, *France* boafted of
her *Melan*, who invented a Sort of Engraving, by which he gave his Figures both
Light and *Shade*, with fingle Strokes only,
without

without ever croffing them : He was alfo a
Painter, and engraved chiefly his own
Works. There was alfo Mr. *Lane,* who
engraved Hiftory and Portraits almoft after
Villamena's Manner; and M. *Rouffellet,*
who engraved the Labours of *Hercules* from
Guido Reni for the *French* King's Cabinet,
in a very beautiful and expreffive Stile, peculiar to himfelf; M. *Anthony Bos,* who
both etched and engraved in a Stile of his
own, did not fucceed fo well; we have of
his Engraving the Figures in all the Books
of M. *Defargue's* Works, who was a Ma-
thematician, Geometrician, and Profeffor
of Perfpective in the Academy at *Paris,*
and in a printed Volume of his Lectures.
In the Time of *Bos,* the famous *Nanteuil*
began to engrave Portraits in a moft beautiful Manner of his own Invention; and
Francis Poilly made himfelf eminent by engraving with great Sweetnefs an infinite
Number of Pieces of Devotion, from the
Works of *Raphael, Caracci, Guido Reni,*
and others; whilft *Cornelius Bloemaert* gain-
ed great Reputation at *Rome,* by engraving
many of the Works of *Peter* of *Cortona,*
and other Mafters, in the moft foft and delicate Stile, that was, perhaps, ever feen
'till his Time; and excited that celebrated
Engraver, *Francis Spierre,* to apply himfelf

B. 6   to

to imitate his fine Manner in the beautiful
Prints which he publifhed; the Out-lines
of which are exceedingly fine, but the Engraving is not fo foft and delicate as *Bloemaert*'s.   M. *Rulet* afterwards engraved at
Rome many beautiful Prints, with the Affiftance of *Ciro Ferri*, from his Defigns, and
was followed by M. *Bodet*, who engraved
in the fame Stile, at *Paris*, for the King's
Cabinet, the four Pictures of *Albano*, which
are in the *Falconieri* Palace at *Rome*.   There
was alfo M. *Vanfculp*, who did many Hiftory Pieces and Portraits with great Sweetnefs; and M. *Maſſon*, who, with *Mignard*'s
Affiftance, engraved the Portrait of the
Count of *Harcourt* from one of his Paintings.   After this, Madam *Claudia Stella*
etched at *Paris* many very fine Prints, by
which fhe not only acquired great Renown,
but almoft put the Male Sex to Shame;
and, among others, this ingenious Lady
did a beautiful one of *Mount Calvary*, from
a celebrated Painting of the famous *Pouſſin*,
which fhe preferved with more Care than
her choiceft Jewels.   Laftly, M. *Edelink*,
a *Fleming*, with the Affiftance of M. *Charles
le Brun*, firft Painter of *Louis* the XIV. engraved his Works in a Stile fomething different from that which M. *Rouſſellet* practifed at *Rome*, but more bold, expreffive,
and

and harmonious: We have alfo of his Engraving, the *Family of Darius,* a Print very
much efteemed in the World, and a *Madonna,* from a Painting of *Raphael,* which
is preferved in the *French* King's Cabinet
of Pictures.

I have here given you an Epitome of the
ufeful Art of Engraving, from its firft Dif-
covery at *Florence,* 'till through a Series of
many Years, it was gradually brought to a
State of Perfection by the fucceffive united
Labours of the great Mafters I have enu-
merated; as any ingenious Lover of this
Art may eafily perceive, by examining and
comparing their Works: And therefore,
though moft Countries in *Europe* have produced many eminent Men of this Profeffion,
fince the Time of *Edelink,* fhall, to avoid
Prolixity, omit them, becaufe few of the
Curious can be unacquainted with their Performances, which have introduced into the
World   a   noble   Emulation   between   the
Graver and the *Pencil,* inafmuch as the Ex-
cellencies, Requifites and Prerogatives of
thefe fine Arts, are nearly the fame, that
is to fay, Defign, Relief, Expreffion of the
Paffions, Multiplicity of the Objects, near
and diftant Profpects of the Country and
Buildings, Delicacy of the Out-lines, and,
I might almoft fay, Colouring itfelf. This,

I believe,

I believe, will evidently appear to all, who attentively examine and reflect on the Works, which thefe Mafters have publifhed, having a due Regard to the Time and Place they lived in, from the Beginning of this Art, to its Perfection, by their united Endeavours, to the common Advantage of all Mankind.

Of

Of ENGRAVING *in General.*

MY Intention, in treating of this noble and ufeful Art, is not fo much
to inftruct the Mafters of this Profeffion, as
to inform the Lovers of it, what are the
Sentiments of the moft eminent Engravers
of the Academy at *Paris*, with regard to
it, and endeavour to infpire the Publick
with a Love for it, by giving them fome
fhort, eafy and ufeful Directions, how to
judge with Certainty of Performances in
this Art.

The Principles, on which this Art is
founded, are the fame as thofe of Painting,
viz. Defign, which an Engraver ought to
be a perfect Mafter of, becaufe, without
it, he will never be able to imitate a Picture, or Defign, with any tolerable Degree
of Perfection ; they may indeed be finely
engraved, but will want both the Juftnefs
of the Out-lines, and beautiful Expreffion
of the Originals.

I fhall pafs over in Silence the Manner
in which an Engraver ought to defign, becaufe it fhould be the fame in which a
Painter does, and only obferve, that he
fhould diligently apply himfelf to defign
Hands and Feet from the antique Statues,

Nature,

Nature, and the Paintings of the beſt Maſters, and that he ought particularly to ſtudy
the Prints of *Auguſtin Caracci* and *Villamena*, who have deſigned thoſe Extremities with great Eaſe and Perfection : ·This
I ſay, that the Engraver may acquire a Facility of doing them with a good *Goût*, and
be able to correct Errors, when he engraves
from the Works of Painters or Deſigners,
who were not perfect in this Branch of
their Profeſſion.

But when he is to copy the Paintings of
eminent Maſters, then he ought entirely to
lay aſide any particular Manner of Deſigning he has acquired, and conform himſelf
to that of the Works he would imitate, in
order to preſerve that Character, which dif-
tinguiſhes the Stile of one Maſter from another ; and to this End, he ſhould deſign
from the Paintings of *Raphael*, *Caracci*,
Dominichino, *Pouſſin*, and others ; and if
he has only an Opportunity of ſeeing them,
and not Time to copy them, he ſhould remark all their particular Beauties, and their
different Manners of forming the Out-lines
of their Figures.

It is very neceſſary alſo, that an Engraver ſhould underſtand *Perſpective* and
Architecture.

Perſpective, by the Degradations of *ſtrong*
and *faint*, enables him with Eaſe to throw
                                    backwards

backwards the Figures and other Objects of the Picture, or Defign, he would imitate; and *Architecture*, to preferve the due Proportion of its feveral Orders, which good Painters very often do not give themfelves the Trouble of doing in their Defigns, which are only done by the Glance of the Eye, and commonly left to the Difcretion of the Engraver.

Of the Quality of COPPER *requifite for* PLATES.

THE Red is the beft, and moft frequently made Ufe of, becaufe it is the *tougheft*, and adheres moft to the Graver; many deceive themfelves, when they heat it to foften it; on the contrary, 'tis better it fhould be a little hard, provided it is not brittle: To prevent which, they need only give Directions to thofe, who prepare the Plates, to hammer them a little cold, and take Care, that they are made perfectly fmooth, without Cavities or Flaws, and of equal Strength throughout.

Before the Engraver begins to trace any Thing on them, although they appear very well polifhed, it will not be improper to take a Burnifher, and rub them well with it, in order to clear them of what the Stone and Fire may have left, which frequently
renders

renders the Bottom of the Engraving foul
and tarnifhed.   As to the Gravers, all Artifts know, that they ought to be made of
the beft and pureft Steel, without any,
Mixture of Iron, and well tempered;
their Form 'tis needlefs to fpeak of, becaufe moft Engravers chufe them according
to their Fancy; however, thofe are beft,
that are of a moderate Length, almoft
fquare, and fmaller at the Point, but Care
muft be taken that they be not too thin,
that they may be able to refift the Work,
without bending or breaking : and the Engraver ought to take particular Care, that
his Inftrument is very fharp, and a little
turned up at the Point, that he may the
more eafily difengage it from the Plate;
and never engrave any Thing with a blunt
Inftrument, if he defires his Work fhould
be neat and fine, for if he does, it will appear as if it was only fcratched.

There are fome who fhew great Facility
in their Engraving, others great Labour;
and fome who affect, in croffing their
Strokes, to form acute Angles, others,
perfect Squares.

Thofe, who have the Facility I fpeak of,
are *Goltzius, Muler, Lucas, Kilian,* and
fome others; whofe principal View in many
of their Performances feems to have been
to fhew the World, by the winding Cuts

of

of their Gravers, that they were Mafters of them; without giving themfelves any Concern about the Juftnefs of the Out-lines, the Expreffion, or the Effects of the Light and Shade, that were in the Picture or Defign they would reprefent.

The Manner of Engraving, which appears to me to be done with great Labour, is that which has an infinite Number of Strokes and Points, confounded together without any Order, which make it look more like a Defign than Engraving.

An Engraver fhould never, in croffing the firft Strokes with the fecond, make very acute Angles, particularly in reprefenting Flefh; becaufe it forms a very difagreeable Piece of *Taby-like Lattice-Work*, which deprives the Eye of that agreeable Repofe, with which it defires to view all Sorts of Objects.

The Squares made by croffing the Strokes fhould never have very acute Angles, except in the Reprefentation of fome Clouds, in Tempefts, and the Waves of the Sea, as alfo in reprefenting the Skins of hairy Animals, and the Leaves of Trees.

The Medium, between Square and Acute, feems to me the beft and moft agreeable to the Eye; as 'tis alfo the moft difficult to do, becaufe the Irregularity of the Strokes is moft perceptible: However, they

they muſt not be quite Square, becauſe that reſembles Stone too much.

FIRST, the Engraver ſhould obſerve the Action of the Figures, and of all their Parts, with their Out-lines ; remark how they advance towards, or recede from his Sight, and conduct his Graver according to the Riſings or Cavities of the Muſcles, or Folds, widening the Strokes in the Lights, and contracting them in the Shades, as alſo at the Extremity of the Out-lines, to which he ought to conduct the Cuts of his Graver, that the Figures or Objects repreſented may not appear as if they were gnawn; and lightning his Hand, that the Out-lines may be perfectly formed without ſeeming ſtiff or cut *. And although he break off his Strokes at the Place where a Muſcle begins, either out of Neceſſity to form it, or to give it greater Expreſſion; yet they ought always to have a certain Connection with each other, ſo that the firſt Stroke ſhould often ſerve to make the ſecond; becauſe this ſhews a Freedom of the Graver, and all Engraving is more or leſs beautiful, in Proportion as it ſeems

* The ingenious *Rouſſellet* excelled in this Reſpect.

free

free and eafy. He ought, however, to take Care, that they always flow freely and naturally, and avoid all odd fantaſtical Windings, which proceed rather from Caprice than Neceſſity; and yet not run into the contrary Extreme, and like many young Artiſts, who, when they have a Mind to engrave *finely*, make none but ſtrait Strokes, becauſe 'tis eaſier to do ſo, than conduct the Graver with Judgment, according to the various Riſings and Cavities of the Muſcles, which they do not well underſtand, becauſe they are ignorant of Anatomy and Deſign.

Directions *for engraving the* Hair *of* Men *and* Beasts, *and the* Beard.

T H E Engraver ſhould begin theſe by making the Out-lines of the principal Locks, and afterwards ſketch out the principal Shades, omitting the great Lights, becauſe they may be covered at Pleaſure, as he finiſhes them, to the very Extremities. They ſhould be ſketched out, as it were, in a careleſs Manner, that is to ſay, with a few careleſs, free, and at the ſame Time, unequal Strokes, to have Room as he finiſhes them, to throw into the void Spaces, which proceed from theſe Inequalities, ſome finer and thinner Strokes. When

When Hair is engraved in this Manner, it appears much more free and natural, than when done otherwife; and indeed, it fhould be exprefled, as far as poffible, particularly when the Figures are not very large, by fingle Strokes only; for which Reafon the Engraver fhould not attempt to throw in any Strokes, when 'tis well exprefled without them; and if he does flip in any on the fhady Side, to mix and unite it the better with the Flefh, they muft be exceedingly fmall and fine.

For SCULPTURE.

IF he has a Mind to reprefent Sculpture, he fhould never make his Work very dark, becaufe, as Statues, *&c.* are commonly made of white Marble, or Stone; the Colour reflecting on all Sides does not produce fuch dark Shades as other Matters do. Neither fhould he make Balls in the Eyes of his Figures, as if he had copied a Painting; or the Hair of the Head and Beard, as it is naturally, which fhews us fome Hairs detached from the reft, and flying in the Air; for it would be reprefenting Things contrary to Truth, becaufe Sculpture cannot do this.

For

For STUFFS.

LInnen fhould be engraved finer and thicker than other Stuffs, it may be with one fingle Stroke, and if they do ufe two, it muft be only in fome fmall Places, and the Shades; to give it a Samenefs, and prevent that Harfhnefs it would otherwife have, when oppofed to, or layed on Drapery and other darker Bodies, which are croffed with many Strokes. If it is white Cloth, it fhould be engraved with Strokes, large or fmall, proportionable to the Finenefs or Coarfenefs of the Stuff reprefented, but with two Strokes only. It may be objected, there are Inftances where 'tis engraved with three; to which I anfwer, thofe who have done fo, fought to be expeditious, and that if the Diverfity of Stuffs can be reprefented by Engraving, it makes the Piece more agreable, but then the Labour is much greater, and more fatiguing. It ought to be obferved, that on all Occafions, when there is a Neceffity of croffing the Strokes, the fecond fhould be finer than the firft, and the third than the fecond; becaufe it makes the Work more foft and mellow.

Stuffs that have a Luftre ought to be engraved with ftronger and ftraiter Strokes than others ; becaufe, as they are commonly of Silk, they produce flat and broken Folds, particularly if it is Sattin, which is ftiff on Account of its Gum : Thefe being expreffed by one or two Sttokes, according to the Lightnefs or Darknefs of their Colours, fhould have finer ones between them.

Velvet and *Plufh* are expreffed in the fame Manner, by fine Strokes between others, only with this Difference ; the firft Strokes. ought to be much ftronger than for Stuffs, and the finer ones between them, fhould hold the fame Proportion to them, as thofe in Stuffs have.

Metals, as Veffels of Gold and Copper, or Armour of polifh'd Steel, are to be engraved in the fame Manner, with fine Strokes between ftrong ones ; it is the Oppofition of Light to Shade, that caufes the Luftre.

For Architecture.

PErfpective fhews us, that the Strokes which form receding Objects, tend to the Point of View ; if a Piece to be engraved contain any entire Columns, it will be proper to reprefent them, as far as can possibly poffibly be done, by perpendicular Lines; becaufe in croffing them according to their Roundnefs, thofe Strokes which are near their Capitals, being oppofed to thofe which are near their Bafis, produce an Effect very difagreeable to the Sight, unlefs they are fuppofed to be at a very great Diftance, which renders the Objects almoft parallel.

For LANDSKIPS.

THOSE, who practife Etching, may form the Out-lines by it, particular-ly of the Leaves of Trees; this is fome-thing more expeditious than Engraving, and does as well, provided it be done with Difcretion, and not too ftrong, and that Care be taken in finifhing it with the Gra-ver, that the Etching be not perceptible, becaufe it has not the Softnefs of Engraving. I think an Engraver cannot do better than conform himfelf to *Auguftin Caracci*'s Man-ner, who etched exceedingly well, but may finifh higher, as Occafion requires; *Villa-mena* alfo, and *John Sadalaer*, etched very well, as likewife *Cornelius Cort*, who did fome Pieces from *Mutian*, which are very fine, and may ferve as Guides to him.

C

For the STROKES *or* CUTS *of the*
GRAVER.

IN the Reprefentation of Objects that
are *fteep*, the firft Strokes fhould be
frequently interrupted and broken off; the
fecond ftrait, cutting the others with acute
Angles, and accompanied with fome long
Points. If Rocks are reprefented, the fecond Strokes fhould not form the Angles
fo acute, as for other Things; becaufe
Flints and Pebbles commonly fhine more
than other Matters.

The Objects receding towards the Horizon ought to be touched very lightly,
and charged with very little Shade, though
the Mafs fhould appear dark, as it may
happen from fome Shades, fuppofed to
proceed from Clouds intercepting the Rays
of the Sun; inafmuch as thefe Shades,
however ftrong they may appear, are always faint, compared to thofe which are
on the Figures and other Bodies in the
Fore-part of the Piece, on Account of the
Diftance and Air that intervenes between
the Objects.

For

For WATER.

ALL Waters are either *calm*, or agitated with *Waves* like the Sea; or by *Cafcades* and *rapid Currents*, like Rivers, &c.

As for the *calm*, they are reprefented by ftrait Strokes, running parallel with the Horizon, with finer ones between them, which are to be omitted in fome Places, to make that fhining Reflection which proceeds from the Water. By the fame fecond Strokes alfo, made more or lefs ftrong, according as the Nature of Things requires; and fometimes by perpendicular ones, the Forms of Objects, either reflected on the Surface of the Water, or advanced at a Diftance on its Banks, are reprefented: obferving that they are to be reprefented *ftrongly* or *faintly*, in Proportion as they approach to, or recede from the Fore-part of the Piece; and if *Trees* are to be reprefented, it fhould be with Out-lines, particularly if they are in the Fore-part of the Piece, and the Water clear, becaufe they are naturally fo reprefented by the Reflection of the Water.

Thofe which are *agitated*, as are the Waves of the Sea, are reprefented by Strokes, bending according to the Agitation of the Water, with finer ones between them, cutting them with very acute Angles.

Lastly, those which fall with Rapidity from Rocks or Precipices, are to be expressed by first Strokes, according to the Nature of the Fall, with finer ones between them, leaving the Lights formed by the Light or Beams of the Sun, falling directly on them, very bright, and the more so, as they approach the Fore-part of the Piece.

For CLOUDS.

WHEN the Clouds appear *thick* and *agitated,* the Graver ought to be turned about, according to their Form and Agitation, and if they produce any dark Shades, which require double Strokes, the second should cut the first with more acute Angles than in Figures, because it gives a certain Transparency very proper for those Bodies, which are only Vapours; but then the first Strokes ought to be stronger than the second.

Flat Clouds, losing themselves insensibly with the Sky, must be formed by Strokes parallel with the Horizon, waved a little, according as they appear more or less thick; and if it be necessary to use second

cond Strokes, they fhould cut the firft with rather acuter Angles than in the former, and the Extremities of them fhould be done with fo light a Hand, as not to form any Out-line.

The *calm, ferene Sky* fhould be expreffed by parallel Strokes, very ftrait, without any Winding.

For *preferving* an EQUALITY *and* HARMONY *in the* WORK.

THE principal Objects of a Piece fhould be wholly fketched out, before any Parts of them are finifhed ; as for Example, if 'tis an hiftorical Piece, containing Groupes of Figures, two or three of the principal ones fhould be fo perfectly defigned, that their Expreffion fhould be as vifible as if they were only intended for Sketches : For if the Engraver waits to perfect the Defigning as he finifhes them, he will frequently miftake; and fometimes not be able to recover himfelf, without defacing the whole, and beginning again, which many will not do, for Fear of fpoiling the Neatnefs of their Engraving, in which they have exerted their utmoft Abilities, thinking the whole Merit of an Engraver confifts in that; which is the Reafon one fees Abundance of Plates finely engraved, but with-

C 3, out

out Expreſſion. If any one objects to this, that it is then uſeleſs to engrave neatly; I anſwer, an Engraver ought, as far as he can, to join Correctneſs and Juſtneſs of Deſign, with Neatneſs of Engraving; but not neglect the former, and place his whole Merit in the enticing Allurements of the latter, which frequently render his Works inſipid and lifeleſs. On the contrary, I would not have him run into the other Extreme, and make his Works faint, but would have them ſtrong and bold; for the Force of a Print does not conſiſt in its Darkneſs, but in the juſt Degradations of Light and Shade, which ought to be more or leſs ſtrong, according as they approach to, or recede from the Sight.

If we examine the Works of eminent Maſters, we ſhall find they are not dark, unleſs they are become ſo through Length of Time; they have perfectly imitated Nature, which is not ſo, particularly in Fleſh, except in *Night Pieces*, where the Objects are repreſented enlightened by Torches or Lamps.

Small Works require finer Engraving than large ones, and in croſſing, the Strokes ſhould form more acute Angles, that the Engraving may not appear ſtiff and dry, notwithſtanding the Figures are ſmall. If the Work requires to be highly finiſhed,

it ought not for that Reaſon to be over laboured, but engraved ſo artfully, as to appear done with Eaſe and Expedition, although it has coſt great Labour and Pains.

Large Works, I mean when the Figures
and Objects are large and bold, require
ſtrong, firm, and bold Strokes, and con-
tinued as much as can be; that is to ſay,
never broken off, but when the Muſcles or
Folds abſolutely demand it: and the Engraver, as I have ſaid before, in theſe, as
well as ſmall Works, ought to endeavour
to perſuade the Spectator, that they were
done with Facility and little Labour.

If it is neceſſary to croſs the Strokes (as
it often is, particularly in the Shades, to
expreſs well the Force and Harmony of a
Painting) they ſhould be croſſed the contrary Way to that they were ſketched, and
the Angles formed by the ſecond Strokes
ſhould be more acute; this contributes
much to the Neatneſs and Life of a Print.

There ſhould never be too much Engraving on the Lights, but they ſhould be
lightly paſſed over, and with few Strokes;
I mean they ſhould be unconfined, and
that the half Shadings, if the Engraver de-
ſires to finiſh to Perfection, ſhould be very
bright; becauſe, if they are very dark,
they deſtroy and hinder the Effect intended
by them, as it will be difficult to find a

Dark-

Darknefs in the Shades fufficient to give them Life and Roundnefs: and if the Engraving is from a Defign taken from a Painting, the Lights and Shades ought to be rather larger than in the Original; becaufe, though it be finifhed ever fo highly, it is never fo exactly done, as the Painting; which for that Reafon requires more Labour and Trouble, on Account of its Colours.

Some may perhaps fay, 'tis impoffible to imitate Colours by Engraving, becaufe we have only *White* and *Black*; when I fpeak of imitating them, I do not pretend to make a Diftinction between *Blue* and *Green*, *Red* and *Yellow*, and the fame of other Colours; but only to imitate their *Maffes*, as *Voftermans*, *Bolfwert*, and fome others have done in their Engravings from *Rubens:* and it is certain, that thofe Works, in which this is done by an ingenious Engraver, will be much more agreeable, and produce a much better Effect. A good Engraver muft therefore, as I have faid, be a very ingenious Man, becaufe he will fometimes meet with *bright* Colours, one upon another, which produce no Effect, but by their Difference, and caufe what is called a *pierced Body*; an Accident, which ought to be carefully avoided, becaufe it deftroys the Intelligence of Light and Shade.

Shade. Care muſt alſo be taken not to ſpoil the principal Lights, by affecting to imitate Colours too much, and particularly of the Figures in the Fore-part of the Piece, becauſe this would prevent their advancing, and entirely thwart the Painter's Intention.

But as *Etching*, or Engraving with *Aqua Fortis*, is at preſent ſo much in Vogue, I find myſelf obliged to tell you, it was never carried to ſuch Perfection, as at this Time. In this, a ſtrong Expreſſion of the Paſſions, a fine Underſtanding of Light and Shade, and beautiful Manner of Engraving, are equally conjoyned, when it comes from the Hand of an ingenious Artiſt, who is able to expreſs himſelf with equal Force and Judgment in all the different Parts of his Profeſſion. I mean that *Etching* which cannot be fine without the Aid of the Graver, which gives it all the Perfection that can be deſired; and which the Ancients have not ſhewn in their Performances of this Kind, becauſe they did not ſo well underſtand the various Graces proper for Painting and Engraving, as the Moderns. However, it will be neceſſary to ſpecify the Properties peculiar to this Art, to enable the Reader to judge of its Merit. By the Means of *Aqua Fortis*, all Subjects are carried even beyond Nature, it acts with

C 5 ſuch

fuch Quicknefs, that it equals the Expedi--
tion of the Pencil, and enables an Artift,
almoft inftantly, to exprefs the Productions
of his Genius with all its Vivacity and
Force; for which Reafon, as 'tis much
more expeditious than the Graver, and its
Manner eafily known, we fee many apply
themfelves to Engraving with it, becaufe
they can exprefs the Sprightlinefs of their
Fancy, with more Freedom and Expedition than with the Graver.

Having treated of the Art of *Engraving*
in general, I think it will not be improper
in this Place to endeavour to obviate fome
Prejudices, which certain Criticks entertain
with regard to it.

The *Firft* is, That 'tis eafy to diftinguifh
thofe Prints that have been engraved by
the Painters themfelves, or by other Painters from their Works.

. The *Second*, That an Engraver by Profeffion can never acquire a Painter's Stile of
Engraving; fo that they pretend to be able
to know by a Print, whether it was engraved by a Painter, or an Engraver by Profeffion.

The *Third* and *Laft*, That the modern
Engravers cannot poffibly exprefs the Works
of the ancient Painters, fo well as thofe
have done, who were their Contemporaries; becaufe, fay they, every Engraver
engraves

engraves according to the *Gusto* of the Time he lives in, and therefore 'tis impofsible for a modern Engraver to exprefs the Works of *Raphael*, in the fame Manner as *Mark Antonio*, *Augustin* of *Venice*, *Sylvester* of *Ravenna*, &c. have done.

After having diligently examined thefe three Opinions, and the Prints in Difpute, it appears to me, that there is more of Prejudice than Reality in them.

For Example, with regard to the *first Opinion*, I have found there are fome Prints engraved by *Simon Cantarini* from *Guido* and *Louis Caracci*, that are preferable to many that were inconteftably engraved by *Guido* himfelf. And as thefe Gentlemen are at Variance amongft themfelves, concerning many of *Guido*'s Prints, which * fome of them affirm were engraved by *Guido* himfelf, and others, by other Hands ; I think this Diverfity of Sentiments fufficiently proves, that their Opinion deferves to be very little relied on.

In Oppofition to the *fecond Opinion, viz. That an Engraver by Profeffion can never acquire a Painter's Stile of Engraving* : There are many Pieces engraved by *Gerard Audran*,

---

* Amongft others, a Print from *Louis Caracci*, engraved by *Simon Cantarini*, reprefenting a Man poffeffed by an evil Spirit, which moft of thefe Critics believe was engraved by *Guido* himfelf.

which,

which, I am perſuaded, if theſe Gentlemen had ſeen without knowing they were done by him, they would rather have thought them the Productions of a Painter than an Engraver; for they are touched with ſo much Life and Judgment, that I much queſtion whether any Painter could have exceeded them. To be convinced of this, they need only look on the *Judges* in the Print of the *Martyrdom of St. Laurence,* from *Le Seur*; on the *Pyrrhus ſaved,* from *Pouſſin*; the *Rape of Truth,* from the ſame; on the *Paſſage of the Red Sea,* from *Verdier,* &c. 'Tis true it may be objected, that the Figures in the Fore-part of theſe Prints have a *Boldneſs* and *Strength* of Engraving, which you do not find in any Piece engraved by Painters; but this is a Perfection their Works have not, and no Way invalidates my Opinion: which is, that theſe Prints have as much *Life* and *Force,* and even more than are to be found in many Prints engraved by Painters themſelves.

To remove this Prejudice, the famous *Bernard Picart* choſe ſeveral Deſigns which had never been engraved; and having privately engraved them, and printed ſome Copies on dirty Paper, he diſperſed them under-hand, and had the Satisfaction to find, that not one of theſe Criticks ever ſuſpected fufpected they were not Prints, which had been engraved and printed in *Italy*. One of thefe Pieces was from *Pouffin*, and only fketched out, as if with a Pen, which many People took for a Defign; another was a fmall *Holy Virgin*, in an Oval, from *Carlo Maratti*, which had been engraved before at *Paris*, almoft as large as the Life, by his Father *Stephen Picart*. Thofe, who had never feen the large Print, thought the fmall one the Work of one of *Guido*'s Difciples, from *Guido*; and thofe, who had feen it, took the fmall one for an Original, engraved by *Carlo Maratti* himfelf. There was alfo a Print of *Rebecca*, which they did him the Honour to attribute, both for the Invention and Engraving, to *Carlo Maratti*. Three other Prints, the one a *Jefuit*; another, a *St. Jerom*; and the third, a *Holy Virgin* on the Clouds: Some thought were done by *Guido* himfelf, and others, by fome of his Difciples.

With regard to the third Opinion, *That the modern Engravers cannot attain the Stiles of the ancient Painters, becaufe they live in another Age, and every Age has, as they pretend, a peculiar Manner*; Thefe Gentlemen do not obferve, that they confound the Manner of Engraving, they are ufed to fee, in thefe old Prints, with the Stile of the Painter; fo that when they fee
a Print

a. Print of one of *Raphael's* Compofitions, with all the Out-lines traced with an equal *black* Stroke, and with a *fine* and *faint* Engraving, without Degradation of *Light* and *Shade*, or *Roundnefs* of the Figures, as all the Engravings of that Time are; they approve of it, as if it was *Raphael's* Manner, which is abfolutely falfe. Thofe, who have it in their Power, have nothing to do, but compare *Mark Antonio's*, or any other Engraver's Prints of that Age, with the original Defigns, as I have done, with regard to many of them; and they will fee, that they have been far from imitating them exactly. They have even taken the Liberty to make Grounds to fome Defigns that had none, and finifh fome Parts, that were but lightly touched, according to their own Fancy. I do not defign to diminifh the Efteem, that is due to the Merit of thofe Prints, but value them as much as any Body, and efteem thofe who engraved them, on two Accounts; firft, becaufe they have preferved us many fine Works, the Originals of which are either loft, or cannot be feen by every Body; and fecondly, becaufe we ought to regard them as the *Inventors* of *Engraving*; and therefore ought to admire, that they were able to carry the Art to fuch Perfection as they did, particularly *Mark Antonio*, and thofe who

who are called *les petits Maitres*, whom we ought to ufe with great Indulgence.

It would be ridiculous to expect from the Inventors of any Art, all the Perfection it acquires in a Series of Years; and it is no lefs ridiculous, in admiring their Works, to fhut our Eyes againft the Dif-coveries that have been made fince their Time. I think it very reafonable, that their Prints fhould bear a better Price than the fine modern ones, not becaufe they are better, but becaufe they are very fcarce, there being but few good Copies of them extant ; but am perfuaded, if one of the fine modern Prints was as rare, and as ancient as thofe of the firft Mafters, it not only would, but ought to bear a better Price than they do. For Example; the ancient Print of *Raphael*'s *Holy Family*, taken from a Painting in the *French* King's Cabinet, is, in my Opinion, infinitely in-ferior to that engraved by Mr. *Edelink* ; and yet there are *Virtuofi*, who have the ancient one, and difdain to look on Mr. *Edelink*'s, dut of meer Obftinacy, becaufe they will efteem nothing but what is ancient and fcarce.

Gentlemen, who know the intrinfick Value of Works, can hardly conceive that Prejudice can go fo far ; and indeed the Dealers in Prints themfelves are to be
chiefly

chiefly blamed for it, for as very few Lovers of Prints are competent Judges of them, and therefore rely on what they fay, they out of a mercenary View infpire them with a Contempt for modern Prints, becaufe they are eafily to be had, and are continually filling their Ears with the Merit of thofe Pieces, which are very rare, and confequently not always to be purchafed. Mr. *Picart* gives us an Inftance of this, which I will relate in his own Words : " One *Pefne*, an excellent Defigner on Paper, but very indifferent Engraver, engraved the *feven Sacraments* of *Pouffin*, each on two Plates. After a certain Number of them had been work'd off, and difperfed in the World, *Gerard Audran*, having bought the Plates, with *Pefne*'s Defigns of them, retouched, and mended them from the faid Defigns, and made them incomparably better than they were before. *Gerard Audran*'s Merit is fo well known, that it needs no Recommendation ; neverthelefs, a Dealer in Prints (at *Paris*) had the Affurance one Day, offering to fell me one of the firft Copies, to fay ; *Thefe are fine, thefe are not thofe that were retouched by Audran.* And thus it is thefe mercenary Wretches prepoffefs the Minds of young Gentlemen, who by frequenting the Company

of

of others, who have been imbued with the fame Prejudices, are fo confirmed in them, that they are not afterwards to be undeceived, even though a more equitable *Connoiffeur* fhould undertake to do it; becaufe they think it a Sort of Shame to abandon an Opinion, which they have for many Years believed true, and defended."

But this is no new Prejudice, we find, as I have remarked in the Life of *Henry Goltzius*, there were fome Criticks in his Time, who laboured under it, and were not lefs mortified, when they found themfelves impofed on, by that great Mafter's Imitation of the Stiles of *Albert Durer*, *Lucas* of *Leyden*, &c. than thofe were, whom *Bernard Picart* deceived in the following Manner, which I will alfo give you in his own Words: " To undeceive fome who were prepoffeffed with an Opinion, that the modern Engravers could not reprefent the Works of *Raphael* fo well as thofe did, who were his Contemporaries, I was obliged to engrave fome Prints, which had been engraved before by fome of the ancient Mafters, as by *Mark Antonio*, or fome other; but the Difficulty was to find the Originals, from whence they had engraved them: At laft, by Accident, I had the good Fortune to meet with two of them, and after having examined and compared

compared them with the Prints, which
had been formerly made from them, I
found fo great a Difference between them,
that I did not think myfelf incapable of
fucceeding better, and accordingly re-en-
graved them, to fee if I could not approach nearer the original Defigns, than
my Predeceffors had done."

The *Firft* was a *Venus, who touches one
of Cupid's Arrows, and fhews, that fhe feels
the Effects of the Touch at her Heart:* This
I engraved exactly like the Defign, without Ground, or any Addition.

The *Second* was a *Bacchanal,* which had
been formerly engraved by *Auguftin* of *Venice.* The Defign, from whence I did it,
is certainly the fame from which *Auguftin*
of *Venice* engraved it; the Strokes are the
fame, the Size the fame, and one fees that
the Out-lines of the Figures are exactly the
fame, but the Mufcles within are quite
different. The *Satyrs* have Crowns of
Ivy on their Heads, which, in the old
Print, are like *Cuttings* or *Slips;* the ancient *Engraver* has made *fmall white Leaves,*
all of the fame Form, ranged on a *Ground*
equally *dark;* whereas, in the Defign,
they are *Leaves carelefly* difpofed, which
form a *Mafs of Light,* on a *Light.* There
is a Child, the back Part of whofe Head
you fee, the *Hair* of which refembles *little
Iron*

Iron Hooks ranged round it. The *Hair* of the Head, Skin and Beard, are all *extremely ſtiff*, and *equally black*, which are not ſo in the Deſign, where the Maſſes of Light and Shade are obſerved. For Example, the Belly of *Silenus*, in the old Print, has *Wrinkles* as *dark* as poſſible, and between his *Paps* are three or four Things that look like *Laces* to tie them together, which one knows not what to make of. Laſtly, if any one will give himſelf the Trouble to examine the whole, Part by Part, he will find there is not one of them exact. Nay, even without having the Original before him, he need only have a juſt Idea of the Conſtruction of the *human Body*, to judge, that *Raphael* could never have acquired the Reputation he juſtly has, if his Works were like thoſe ancient Prints; becauſe he would have been inferior to many Painters, who are much inferior to him. I cannot then comprehend, how theſe Gentlemen will perſuade us this is the *true Stile* of *Raphael*; and that it is impoſſible to engrave his Works at preſent, as the ancient Engravers did. For, ſuppoſing a modern Engraver is a Maſter of the Art of Engraving, and can give Figures *Roundneſs*, and the Degradations of *Light* and *Shade*; why cannot he expreſs a Picture, or Deſign, where all theſe are obſerved, ferved, I do not fay as well, but better than the ancient Engravers, who had neither that Freedom of Hand, which the good modern ones have, nor underftood how to give Figures *Roundnefs*, or the Degradations of *Light* and *Shade?* Thofe Engravers might poffibly underftand, *Defigning on Paper* very well; but admitting that, it is ftill certain, they had not Freedom of Hand enough to trace with the Graver what they would on Copper; and that nothing hinders the modern Engravers from being as good Mafters of *Defign* as they were. And 'tis to no Purpofe to alledge, that all Ages do not produce *great Genius's*; for it does not require a *fuperior Genius*, as it does to compofe, or produce Things of their own Invention: Every Body knows, that all Ages have produced very good *Copiers*; and that is all is requifite in the prefent Cafe.

But thefe Gentlemen's Prejudices do not only extend to the Prints from *Rapael*'s Works; they pretend alfo to draw Confequences from them, for thofe from *Rubens*. It cannot be denied, but that they are in this Refpect, in Part, much more in the Right; for the Prints of *Bolfwert*, *Voftermans*, *Pontius*, and *Soutman*, are fo well engraved, and have fo much of the Painter's Stile in them, that I do
not

not think they can be exceeded; and in •
this, *Rubens* has been more happy than
Raphael. But there are many other Prints
engraved from the Works of *Rubens* by
other Engravers of that Age, which are
very ill done, and which thefe Gentlemen
hunt after, whilft they defpife others engraved by Mafters of this Age, though infinitely more in the Stile of *Rubens.* In
this they are to blame ; for, I believe, there
are Engravers now living, who can copy
his Works as well as the beft of his Time,
and much better than the others.

The Reafons I have here affigned, I
think fufficient to convince thofe, who are
defirous to be undeceived ; but if not, I
fhall not defift from my Opinion ; being
perfuaded it proceeds more from my In-
capacity to eftablifh it, than from the Fal-
fity of my Maxims, which I leave to fome
other more ingenious Artift to juftify.

THE

THE
ART *of* ENGRAVING
WITH
AQUA FORTIS.

SECT. I.

To make the hard Varnish for engraving with
Aqua Fortis.

TAKE five Ounces of Greek
Pitch, or (for Want of that) Bur-
gundy-Pitch, five Ounces of Ro-
fin of Tyre, or *Colofonium*, or (for Want of
that) ordinary Rofin : Melt them together
over a gentle Fire in a very clean new
earthen Pot, well varnifhed, or leaded.
Thefe two Things being firft melted, and well mixt together, put into them
four Ounces of the beft Nut Oil; mix
them

them well together over the fame Fire
for a full half Hour, and let them
boil well; then let this Mixture cool a little over a gentle Fire; and afterwards,
touching it with the End of your Finger,
it will rope (if it be boiled enough) like a
glewy Syrup. Then take the Pot from
the Fire, and (the Varniſh being a little
more cooled) ſtrain it though a fine Linnen Cloth, or Taffata, into a well varniſhed earthen Pot; or elſe put it into a
thick Glaſs Bottle, or any other Thing that
will not drink it up, and ſtop it well. Varniſh thus made will laſt twenty Years, and
it will be the better the longer it is kept.

S E C T. II.

To make the Compoſition of Tallow and Oil,
to cover thoſe Places in the Plate, where
you would not have the Aqua Fortis *to*
eat in.

TAKE a well glazed earthen Pipkin, that will hold about a Pint,
put into it half a Pound of hard
Tallow, a Wine Glaſs of Olive Oil, together with a Spoonful of Lamp Black, ſet
it on the Fire, and, as the Tallow diſſolves,
keep ſtirring it with a ſmall Stick, that the
Lamp Black and Oil may the better incorporate;

porate; let it boil the Space of ten or
twelve Minutes; then take a Pencil and
dip it in, and let a Drop or two fall on
a Plate, or any cold hard Thing; and if
the Drops be a little hardened and firm, it
sheweth that the Mixture is well made.
If it is too liquid, 'tis becaufe there is too
much Oil; and then you muft put in more
Tallow; and for the fame Reafon, if too
hard, you muft put in more Oil.

The Reafon why you melt the Oil and
the Tallow together, is to make the Tallow more liquid, and not cool too faft:
For fhould you melt the Tallow alone,
you fhall no fooner take it up with the
Point of your Pencil to carry it to the
Place where you would ufe it, but it will
grow cold.

Put in a greater Quantity of Oil in Winter, than in Summer.

S E C T. III.

To prepare the Ingredients for making the
Aqua Fortis *for the hard Varnifh.*

T H E *Aqua Fortis* is made of Vinegar,
Salt Armoniack, Bay-Salt, and Vert
de Griz.

The

. The Vinegar muſt be of the beſt Sort of White-wine ; but if diſtilled, it is the better, and not ſo ſubject to break up the Varniſh.

The Salt Armoniack muſt be clear, tranſparent, white, pure, and clean.

The Bay-Salt muſt be alſo pure and clean.

The Vert de Griz muſt be clean, and free from any Scrapings of Braſs.

The Salt Armoniack, and Vert de Griz, are commonly ſold at the Druggiſts.

SECT. IV.

To make the Aqua Fortis.

TAKE three Pints of Vinegar, ſix Ounces of Salt Armoniack, ſix Ounces of Bay-Salt, and four Ounces of Vert de Griz ; or of each according to this Proportion, as you will make your Quantity more or leſs ; put them all together in an earthen Pot well varniſhed, large enough, that it may not boil over : Cover the Pot, and ſet it over a quick Fire, and let it boil up two or three Times, and no more : When you perceive it ready to boil, and not before, uncover the Pot, and ſtir it with a little Stick ſometimes, and take heed that it do not

boil

boil over : Having let it boil up two or
three Times, take the Pot from off the
Fire, and let it cool ; but keep the Pot
covered, and when it is cold, pour it into
a Glafs Bottle, and let it ftand ftopped a
Day or two before you ufe it ; and if you
fhall find it too ftrong in the Etching,
pour into it a Glafs or two of the fame
Vinegar you made it of.

S E C T. V.

To know good Copper from bad.

COPPER is better for graving than
Brafs, either with a Graver, or *Aqua
Fortis* ; becaufe Brafs is too brittle. That
Copper is beft, which is free from Flaws,
and not too hard, which you may perceive by its yellowifh Colour, almoft like
Brafs ; and if it be too foft, you may eafily
perceive it by its too great Pliablenefs in
Bending. When you make ufe of it, you
will perceive (in that which is good) a
firm, yet eafy Force in the Entring of
your Graver, on the Backfide of your
Plate ; and that Copper which is beft for
graving, is alfo beft for etching.

SECT. VI.

To planish and polish the Plate.

HERE in *England* you muſt buy your Copper ready forged from the Braſiers. If in *London*, there are People who term themſelves Copperſmiths, and prepare the Plates for immediate Uſe, either large or ſmall, at a fix'd Price *per* Pound.

It is not neceſſary, that they, who deſire to engrave, ſhould forge and poliſh their Copper Plates themſelves; but becauſe in divers Places they cannot conveniently be had ready poliſhed, I have thought fit to ſet down the Manner how they may be done.

Thoſe Plates, which you intend to forge and planiſh, muſt be full as thick as an Half-Crown, becauſe in their forging and planiſhing they will become ſomewhat thinner. You muſt planiſh your Copper cold, as the Silverſmiths do their Plate: And the more it is beaten, or planiſhed with a Hammer, the firmer it is, and leſs ſubject to Holes or Flaws.

Your Plate being well planiſhed, make choice of the ſmootheſt Side for poliſhing: Before you begin to poliſh it, fix it upon
a Board;

a Board ; and when you polish it, let your Board (to which the Plate is fixed) stand a little sloping.

To polish your Plate, take a Piece of a Grinding-stone about the Bigness of your Fist, and fair Water ; rub it firm, and even all over ; and in your Rubbing throw Water often on it, and continue so doing, till you cannot perceive any Dents, Flaws, or Marks of the Hammer : Then wash it clean with Water. Afterwards take a good Pumice-Stone, and some Water, and rub the Plate with it till there appears none of the rough Strokes, or Marks of the Stone : Then wash it clean with Water, as you did before.

Again, do the same Thing with a fine smooth Hone and Water, till all the Marks of the Pumice-Stone are quite rubbed out : This done, wash it clean with fair Water.

Then choose out a smooth Charcoal, without any Knots, or rough Grain, and put it in a well-kindled Fire : Let it be there, till you perceive it red hot ; then take it out of the Fire, and quench it in Water ; then take it out, and pare off the outermost Rind, and rub your Plate with it, and Water, till all the small Strokes of the Hone are rubbed out. If the Coal be bad, it will only slide upon the Plate, and not rub out the

Strokes. This done, dry the Plate; then it is requifite to have it burnifhed over, which Operation is performed by an Inftrument made of well-harden'd polifhed Steel, fomewhat roundifh, termed a Burnifher, with which you rub Plate over, (firft dropping on it fome Drops of Olive Oil,) whereby the Pores of the Copper are the better clofed, and the Scratches of the Charcoal (as there always will remain fome few) effaced.

After the Plate is burnifhed, take a clean Linnen Rag, and rub off the Oil; then take fine Powder of Chalk, and lay it on the Plate, and with another Piece of fine clean Linnen Rag rub it over the Plate, then brufh off the Chalk, and with a third clean Rag rub the Plate over again, and likewife round the Edges, taking Care there be not the leaft Appearance of Oil, or Chalk, left: which being done, take a fmall Piece of Paper, double it in four, as large as the Chops of your Hand-vice; the Ufe of it being to prevent the Teeth of the Hand-vice marking the Copper; put the Paper on the Edge of your Plate, as much above it as below; then apply your Hand-vice, and take Care to fkrew it faft, that the Plate may not flip; this done, your Plate is fitly prepared to lay on your Varnifh.

SECT.

S E C T. VII.

To apply the hard Varnish on the Plate, and make it black.

TAKE your Plate thus cleanfed, and lay it on a Chafing-Difh with a little clear Charcoal Fire in it, and when it is indifferently hot, take it away, and take up fome of the Varnifh with a little Stick, and put a Drop of it on the Top of one of your Fingers ; then lightly touch the Plate with the Top of your Finger in feveral Places at equal Diftances ; as the uppermoft Figure in the Plate, marked with the Letter O, fhews you ; and lay no more on one Place than on another. And if your Plate grow cold, heat it again as before, carefully keeping it from Duft or Filth. This done (having well wiped the flefhy Part of the Palm of your Hand) tap it upon the Plate, till all the little Spots of Varnifh are equally fpread upon the Plate.

After this tapping, wipe or flide your Hand upon the Varnifh, to make it more fmooth and equal ; take great Care that there be not too much Varnifh upon the

Plate, and that your Hand be not fweaty;
becaufe the Sweat mixing with the Varnifh, will caufe little Bubbles, when it is
applied to the Fire, which will become
little Holes in the Varnifh.

Your Varnifh being thus fmoothed upon
the Plate, the Way to black it is this.
Take a great Tallow-candle lighted, that
burns clear; let it have but a fhort
Snuff; then place your Plate againft the
Wall, (firft driving two fhort Nails for it
to reft on,) with the varnifhed Side down-
ward, as the lower Figure in the Plate
reprefents it. Take heed that your
Fingers do not touch the Varnifh; then
take your Candle, and apply the Flame to
the Varnifh, as clofe as you can without
touching the Varnifh with the Snuff of the
Candle; guide the Flame all over, till you
fee it perfectly black; then keep it from
Duft or Filth till it be dried; by fetting
it on the Ground, the Hand-vice uppermoft, bearing againft the Wall, the Bottom of the Plate four or five Inches from
it, and the varnifhed Side innermoft.

'SECT.

SECT. VIII.

To dry and harden the Varnish upon the Plate.

KIndle a Fire in a Chimney with such Charcoal as is not subject to sparkle, and when it is well kindled, range it in a Square, somewhat larger than your Plate, as the Letter P shews you. Before you place your Plate to be dried, hang up a Cloth in the Chimney to prevent any Soot or Filth from falling down upon it, as you may see by the Letters B C D. Then take your Plate and place it in the middle of the Range upon two low Andirons, as the Letter O directs: This done, you will soon perceive the Varnish to smoke ; and when you perceive the Smoke begins to abate, then take the Plate from off the Andirons, and with a Stick (pointed) scratch near the Side of your Plate ; and if it easily takes off the Varnish, you must lay it again upon the Andirons for a little Time ; take it off, and touch it again with your pointed Stick, and if the Varnish comes not off easily, then take it from the Fire, and let it cool.

D 5   If

If the Varnifh do much refift the Point
of the Stick, then prefently throw on fome
cold Water on the Backfide of the Plate,
to cool it, that the Heat of the Plate
may not caufe the Varnifh to be too hard
and brittle.

If your Plate be not very large, a Chafing-Difh, with clear Charcoal in it, will
ferve to harden your Varnifh, taking care
to keep your Room free from any Duft,
and wrap a Cloth or Paper round your
Hand-vice to prevent the Heat coming to
your Hand: But if your Plate fhould be
large, the former Manner is beft, putting
another Hand-vice at the oppofite End;
always having one to help you.

S E C T. IX.

*To choofe the Needles, wherewith to make the
Tools to etch with.*   Plate 3.

CHoofe fome broken Needles of feveral Sizes and Bignefs, fuch as break
neat without bending, and of a fine Grain.
Then take round Sticks of a good firm
Wood, not apt to fplit, of the Length of
half a Foot, or little lefs, of the
Thicknefs of a good large Quill: At the
Ends of which Sticks fix in your Needles,
fo that they ftand out of the Sticks about

as

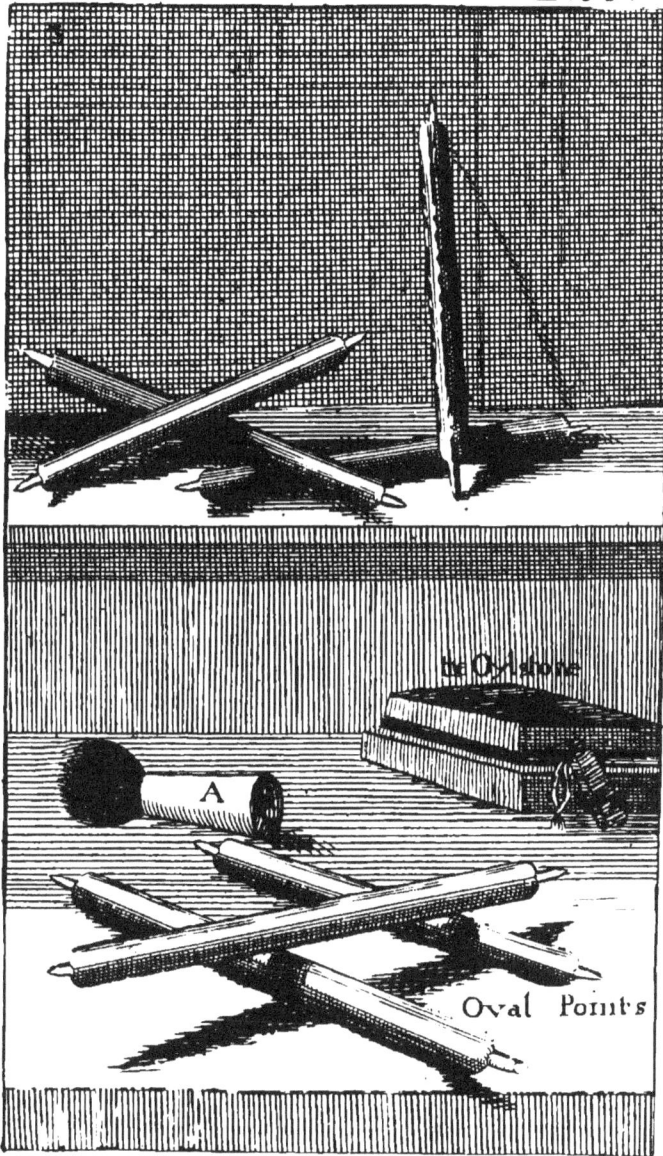

the Oyl stone

A

Oval Points

as much as you fee in the following Figure ; or ftick your Needles in Pieces of Cane of that Length, taking care to put them in the Centre, and leaving about half an Inch out.

S E C T. X.

To whet the Points of the Needles.

THERE are two Ways of whetting your Needles, the one round, the other floping.

You muft have an Oil-ftone with a fine Grain, to whet your Needles upon : Thofe you would have to be round, you muft whet their Points fhort, by rubbing them on the Edge of your Oil-ftone, from one End of the Hone to the other, turning them continually round, as the Figure fhews you. The other, which you intend to make floping, firft make blunt, then holding it firm and fteady, whet it floping upon one Side only, till it come to a fhort roundifh Oval; for the long Oval is not fo good to work with.

You will need a foft Brufh-pencil to wipe off the Varnifh, which the Strokes of your Needle raife up in working, as is reprefented by the Letter A.

D 6   S E C T.

S E C T. XI.

To preserve the Varnish upon the Plate.

YOUR Plate being varnished, place it on a large square Board, and raise up the End from you, so that it may form a Desk, but take care not to raise it too high, left your Plate slide down; some chuse to lay the Plate flat on a Table :———— Lay a Sheet of clean Cartridge Paper under your Plate, and when you work, put upon it a clean Silk or Linnen Hand-kerchief, or a large Piece of clean Wash-leather, to rest your Hand upon, to keep it from the Varnish.

When you have Occasion to use your Ruler, to draw straight Lines, take two Pieces of clean Writing Paper, folded several Times double, about six Inches long, and half an Inch in Breadth; lay these on your Plate, one at each End, of the Length of the Lines you intend to draw; then place your Ruler on these Pieces of Paper, and take care that the Inside of the Ruler does not touch the Varnish; if it should, make your Pieces of Paper thicker, to prevent your Ruler's damaging the Varnish, and take care to keep your Plate free

from

from Filth or Duſt, by bruſhing it now and
then with a Feather.

S E C T. XII.

To etch.

IN etching, you will have Occaſion to
make divers Sorts of Lines or Hatches,
ſome bigger, ſome ſmaller, ſome ſtraight,
ſome crooked. To make theſe, you muſt
uſe ſeveral Sorts of Needles, bigger or
ſmaller, as the Work requires. The great
Lines are made theſe three ſeveral Ways.

1. By leaning harder on the Needle, the
Point being ſhort and thick, makes a large
Paſſage; but the Point being round, it will
not cut the Varniſh clear.

2. By making divers Lines or Hatches,
very cloſe one to another, and then by
paſſing them over again with a thicker
Needle; but this Way is both tedious,
and difficult.

3. By making the Lines with an indifferent big Needle, and letting the *Aqua
Fortis* lie the longer on it. Thoſe Needles, which you whet ſloping with an
Oval, are the beſt to make the large Lines
with, becauſe with their Sides, they cut
what the round Points cannot. Pl. 4.

S E C T.

SECT. XIII.

To guide the Needle on the Plate.

YOU may perceive from what is said, that those Points which you intend to make use of, for graving with *Aqua Fortis*, ought to be whetted exactly round, that they may turn more freely upon the Plate. Some of those round Points must be whetted very sharp, that they may cut the Varnish and Copper easily. If you find that your Point cuts not freely and smoothly, 'tis because it is not whetted exactly round.

If you have Occasion to make your Lines or Hatches of an equal Bigness from one End to the other, whether they be straight or crooked, as those two Lines in the Letters A B represent, you must, as Reason will tell you, lean on your Point with an equal Force from one End to the other.

If you would make your Strokes thicker at one End than at the other, as the second Letters A B shew you, then you must lean on your Point with your Hand harder at the Beginning, and by Degrees lighter and lighter towards the End.

If

4

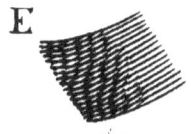

If you would have your Strokes to be such as are reprefented in the third Figure, marked alfo *a b*, that is to fay, larger in the Middle than at either End; you muft lean gently at the Beginning, and then by Degrees harder and harder, till you come to the Middle, and then again lighter and lighter till you come to the End.

Thefe three Sorts of Lines or Hatches, may indifferently ferve for all manner of hatching your Shadows, in any Defign whatfoever, as appears in the Figures, M N, O P, Q G R, T E V; wherein is manifeft, that Shadowing is only a Reiteration of the fame Strokes clofe to one another.

If you defire that your etching with *Aqua Fortis* fhould look as like graving as may be, you muft lean hard upon your Needle in thofe Places where you would have the Lines appear deep and large; that is, fo hard, that the Needle may make fome Impreffion in the Copper. And for the fame Reafon you are to lean very light on thofe Places, which you would have appear faint and fmall.

If it happens that you have made fome Lines, or Hatches too fmall, and are defirous to inlarge your Stroke, you muft pafs it over again with a round fhort Point,

of

of fuch a Thicknefs as you defire your Line fhould be of ; and lean ftrong and firm on thofe Parts of the Line, which you would have large and deep.

If at any Time, by Reafon of the large Lines or Hatches, which you were to make, you have ufed an oval Point (which is the beft to cut the Varnifh) you muft afterwards, with one of your large Needles whetted fhort and round, pafs in the midft of the faid Strokes firmly and ftrongly, but efpecially in thofe Places which you would have large and deep.

S E C T. XIV.

To ufe the Oval Points, to make large Strokes, in etching or graving with Aqua Fortis. Plate 5.

YOU may fee in the Figure A B C D the Form of thofe oval Points, that Part next to C defcribes the End of them; and B D their Sides. They are held, much as you hold a Pen, only the flat Side whetted is ufually held towards the Thumb, as is reprefented in Figure iii. Not but that it may be ufed otherwife, with the Face of the Oval turned towards the middle Finger, as is fhewn in Figure iv. But I have
found

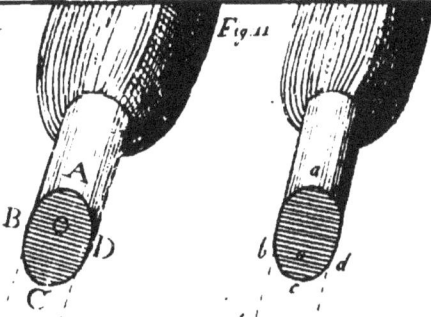

Fig: I

Fig: II

A
B O D
C

a
b x d
c

Fig. III

s
n
r

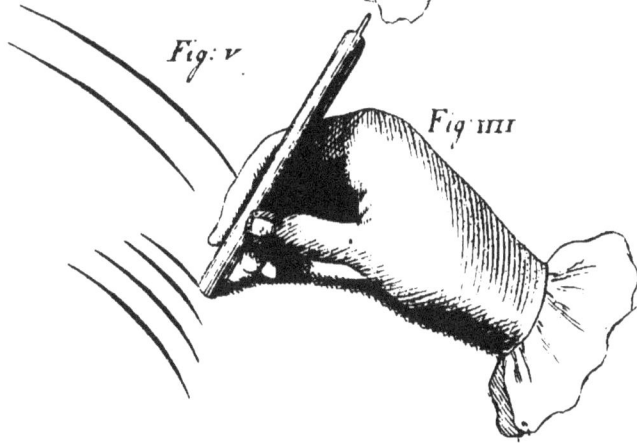

Fig: V

Fig: IIII

found the other Manner to be much better, becaufe you may that Way inforce your Strokes with more Strength and Firmnefs.

To fhew you how to make your Strokes large and deep, and that thefe oval Points are the moft proper for it, take Notice of the two upper, firft and fecond Figures, which are purpofely made the larger, that you may the better apprehend what fhall be hereafter fpoken of them. Your own Reafon will tell you, that if you lean lightly in making your Strokes, thofe Strokes will accordingly be lefs deep, fmaller, and more faint; for the harder you lean, the deeper and larger your Strokes will be. Of this you have an Example in the third Figure marked *r n s*; where leaning lightly at the Beginning, *viz. r,* and then harder by Degrees to *n,* and afterwards lighter by Degrees to *s,* you make your Stroke bigger or fmaller according to your leaning on it, as you find reprefented in the faid third Figure.

But if you would have your Strokes come very fmall and delicate at the End, then with the Point of your fmall Needle lengthen out your Stroke, as you find it reprefented in the two Strokes of the fifth Figure.

Some-

Some will firſt make their Stroke with a round Needle, and then paſs it over again with an oval Point, to inlarge it in thoſe Places, which they would have deeper and bigger ; but the other is the beſt Way.

They that know how to engrave, after they have done etching their Lines with *Aqua Fortis*, may, with the Aſſiſtance of their Graver, make them neater and deeper.

I think it not amiſs, to adviſe you, that in making your Strokes, with your oval Points, you muſt hold them as upright and ſtraight in your Hand as you can, and accuſtom yourſelf to ſtrike your Strokes firm and bold, for that will contribute very much to their Neatneſs and Clearneſs. To do this the better, you muſt be very careful to have your Points always well whetted.

In thoſe Places which you would have appear in your Piece by Way of Landſkip, or the furtheſt Diſtance from the Sight, and in thoſe Places, which approach neareſt the Light, you muſt uſe a very ſlender Point, leaning ſo lightly with your Hand, as to make a ſmall faint Stroke. But when you come to thoſe Places, which you would have more ſhadowed, lean ſo much the harder, that when you come to eat in with your *Aqua Fortis,*

Fortis, you may cover moft of your faint Places at one and the fame Time; for you muft know that thofe Strokes, which you lean lighteft on, do little more than raife up the Varnifh. • So when you apply your *Aqua Fortis* to etch it, it will appear much fainter, than in thofe Places where you have leaned with greater Force, though the Strokes are done with one and the fame Needle. Infomuch, that when you fhall have covered the greateft Part of your faint Places with your Mixture, thofe Places, whereon you leaned ftrongeft, will appear deepeft, though they were all covered at the fame Time. In your working be careful to brufh off all the Duft which you make with your Needles.

You muft provide yourfelf with fome good white Picture-Varnifh, keep it clofe ftopp'd in a Vial, and when you have Occafion to correct any falfe Stroke, or alter any fmall Object, take a fine clean Camel's-Hair Pencil, dip it into the Varnifh, and mix up fome Lamp-Black with it, on a Piece of Glafs, or Oyfter-Shell, (but take care it be not too liquid) which will withftand the *Aqua Fortis,* and is much better for ftopping up fmall Parts, than the Tallow; after it is dry, you
may

may work over it, which cannot be done on the Tallow.

S E C T. XV.

To prepare the Plate, to receive the Aqua Fortis.

YOUR Plate being finished and ready for the *Aqua Fortis,* brush off all the Rubbish and Dust that is in the Strokes. And if there happen to be any Strokes which you would not have the *Aqua Fortis* eat into, or any Places where the Varnish is rubb'd off, then melt your Mixture of Oil and Grease which you have made, and with a Pencil, bigger or smaller, according to the Proportion of those Places which you would mend, cover those Places indifferently thick, and the *Aqua Fortis* will not eat in.

This done, take a Brush or Pencil, and dip it into the said Mixture of Oil and Grease, and rub the Back-Side of you Plate all over, to prevent the *Aqua Fortis* from eating any Part of it; but take heed that your Mixture be not too thin or liquid, for if it be, when you pour your *Aqua Fortis* on the Plate, it will force it from those Places whereto you had applied it.

When

When you find the Mixture begin to grow cold, then put fome fmall Quantity of it on your left Hand, thereby to keep it warm, to be ufed as Occafion fhall require.

In the Winter Time efpecially, when the Weather is cold and moift, before you apply your *Aqua Fortis* to the Plate, it will not be amifs to warm it gently by the Fire, to dry up the Moifture, which the Plate is fubject to by Reafon of the Diftemperature of the Weather. Nay, if it be not warmed, it may likely endanger the breaking up of the Varnifh, at the firft pouring of the *Aqua Fortis* upon the Plate.

S. E C T. XVI.

To make the Trough and Frame to hold the Plate, when you would pour the Aqua Fortis *on it.*

THE Figure oppofite hereto, reprefents both Trough and Frame. The Letter A is one intire Piece of Elm or Oak, of about four Inches thick, and fix Inches broad, or may be of fuch a Length as you fhall think fitteft for your Ufe. You muft cut this Piece of Wood into the Fafhion of a Trough, as the Figure fhews you, making it a little deeper in the Middle,

dle, that the Water running thither, may fall through a Hole made there for that Purpose. Set this upon an Eafel, as the Figure fhews you.

Under the Hole in the Trough, place an earthen Pan well leaded on the Infide, as you fee in Figure B; and therein put your *Aqua Fortis*, let it not ftand too much below the Trough.

The Figure M N O P is one intire Board, of an indifferent Largenefs, as you may judge by the Figure. About both the Sides and Top of this Board, you muft faften a Ledge, about two Inches broad, to keep the *Aqua Fortis* from running off from the Sides, when you pour it in. The Infide of this Board and Trough muft be covered or primed over with a thick Oil-colour, to hinder the *Aqua Fortis* from eating or rotting the Board. Place the lower End of this Board in the Trough floping againft your Eafel, and you muft fix feveral Pegs of Wood or Nails in the Board, to reft your Plate on.

The Figure Q defcribes a little earthen Pot well leaded on both Sides, which you muft have to take up your *Aqua Fortis* out of the Pan, and to pour it on the Plate.

S E C T.

S E C T. XVII.

The Manner of casting the Aqua Fortis *upon
the Plate; and to cover the Places that are
faintest, and most remote from the Eye, with
the fore-mentioned Mixture, as Occasion requires.*

HAVING observed the Way of
placing the Plate for the receiving
of the *Aqua Fortis,* there remains only to
consider the Method you are to follow
in pouring it on, as Occasion requires;
for in some Works, it will be necessary to
pour it on several Times, for the Reasons
hereafter mentioned. Having a sufficient
Quantity of *Aqua Fortis* in your Pan, fill
your earthen Pot, and pour it upon your
Plate, beginning at the Top, and moving
your Hand equally, so that it may run all
over the Plate alike, taking great heed that
the Pot touch not the Plate. Having thus
poured it eight or ten Times, the Plate being
in the Posture expressed in the preceding
Figure, you must turn it crofs-ways, as is
represented in the upper Part of the following Figure, marked C; and pour on it as
it lies that way, ten or twelve Times again,
as before : This done, turn your Plate suit-
ably to the Posture expressed by the
lower

lower Part of the aforefaid Figure, that is to fay, corner-ways, and as it lies fo, pour thereon eight or ten Times; pouring the *Aqua Fortis* thus, at feveral Times, for the Space of half a Quarter of an Hour, more or lefs, according to the Strength of the Water, and Nature of the Copper. For if the Copper be brittle and hard, there muft be the lefs Time allowed for the pouring on the Water; but if foft, the more.

By Chance you may not at the firft be fo well affured of the Strength of your Water, and the true Quality of your Copper; it will therefore not be amifs to give you fome Directions how to know both, that you may proceed according to the Strength or Neatnefs, which you expect to find in your Work. For fome Pieces require more Force, and others more Tendernefs. To know therefore that the Nature of your Copper, and Strength of your Water, are fuch, as the Work you intend requires, pour the *Aqua Fortis* on your Plate, for the Time, as is before mentioned, for the Space of the fourth Part of a Quarter of an Hour. Then take away the Plate, and throw on it a Quantity of fair Water, holding the Pot at a good Height from the Plate, to wafh off the *Aqua Fortis*; for if

it

it be not clean wafhed, the Work will appear green, and confequently you cannot fo well perceive the Operation of your *Aqua Fortis.*

That done, hold your Plate before the Fire, at fuch a Diftance, as that, without melting the Mixture which may be upon it, the fair Water may be dried up. Then take a little Piece of Charcoal, and therewith rub off the Varnifh in fuch Places where the Strokes are faint ; and if you find that the *Aqua Fortis* hath eat deep enough in thofe faint Places, melt your Mixture, and having placed your Plate upon a Defk or Table, take of the faid Mixture, with a Pencil fit for your Work, and cover therewith all thofe Places which you defire fhould be tender, and free from any further Operation of the *Aqua Fortis :* taking great Care that you lay the Mixture thick enough, on the Places which you would have covered ; that is, that the Mixture may fill up the Strokes. And it is at this firft Operation, that you are to cover all the fainteft and fweeteft Places.

Having held your Plate fo long to the Fire that the Moifture is quite taken off (a Thing only neceffary in the Winter Time) put it again upon your Board, and pour on your Water as before, for the Space of about half an Hour, turning your Plate

E   from

from Time to Time, according to the several Postures before expressed. That done, wash off the *Aqua Fortis* with fair Water, as before, and dry your Plate by the Fire, taking especial Care that you melt not the Mixture which you had before put upon it.

Your Plate being dried, put it upon the Desk, or Table, as before, and having melted your Mixture, cover therewith those faint Places and Hatches that are next in Point of Faintness to those that you had covered before. For the different Degrees of Faintness in the Hatches, you have several Examples in the following Figure.

You have been before directed how to guide your Needles and oval Points, and have been told how you are to lean strongly and firmly on the Places where you would have the Strokes be black and deep, and to flack and lighten your Hand where you would have them faint and tender; a Thing which very much facilitates the Operation of the *Aqua Fortis.* For Instance, when you have the first Time with your Mixture covered that Part, which is inclosed by the Line A B C D, and makes a kind of an Oval; you come at the second time, to cover that Space which is between the Line A B C, and the Line E O F; knowing well, that

if

if you have fuffered the *Aqua Fortis* to eat
for the Time requifite, it will have very
near the Effect which you expected.

At the upper End of the Plate, you
have the Form of a Woman's Arm, wherein you may perceive, by the Line marked
a b c d, as alfo by the other, which lies yet
nearer the Shadow, how the fmall Hatches
and fainter Places are ordinarily covered
at two feveral Operations, as Occafion
requires; though, in the forementioned Example of the Arm, once covering may
luckily ferve.

I have alfo thought fit at the Bottom of
the Plate, to fet down four feveral Pieces
of Ground in Landfkip; the firft marked
m m m, is the firft covered, being the
fartheft of all from the Eye; then at another Operation that marked *n n n*; then
that marked *o o o*; there being only that
marked *p*, wherein the *Aqua Fortis* eats in
full and deep.

It may be objected, that the leaning
lightly or hardly on the Points in their proper
Places in working, may make the Strokes
and Hatchings fo, that the *Aqua Fortis*
may eat in anfwerably to your Expectation,
without the Trouble of covering any Places
with your Mixture : To this I anfwer, that
the Work will not altogether have that

E 2 Effect,

Effect, but will be like the fecond Plate, which I have purpofely made after that Manner : For though you can lean harder on fome Places, and lighter on others ; yet the *Aqua Fortis* being poured equally all over the Plate, during the whole Time ; it muft follow, that fome Places will not be fo fweet and tender as they ought, and will come far fhort of that beautiful and lively Continuity, which you perceive in thofe Lines and Strokes where you ufe the Mixture.

If it happen, when you dry your Plate by the Fire to take off the Moifture, as hath been faid before, that the Mixture, for Want of Care, melts and runs into thofe Hatches and Strokes where you would have the *Aqua Fortis* eat further in ; wipe the Place with a foft Cloth, then take the Crumb of ftale Bread, and rub the Place therewith, till fuch Time as you conceive you have taken off all the Greafinefs. This Remedy is only applicable in Cafe of Extremity ; for you are to obferve, that it is impoffible to take out the Greafe fo clearly, but that it will fomewhat hinder the Operation of the *Aqua Fortis.* And therefore there muft be the more Care taken to prevent it.

Having

Having thus covered your Places as Occafion requires, for the fecond Time, place your Plate on the Board aforefaid, and pour your *Aqua Fortis* on it, for another half Hour.

That done, wafh it with Water, and dry it as formerly, and cover the Places you think require it ; for the third Time, you muft know, that the faint Places are to be proportionable to, that is, more or lefs, according to the feveral Defigns' and Pieces you work upon. When this is done, pour your *Aqua Fortis* upon it, for the laft Time, and it is at this Operation, that you are to beftow more or lefs Time, than in the former, according to the Nature of your Work.

For Inftance, if there be in your Plate fuch Hatches and Shadows, as require much Depth and Fulnefs, which confequently will be very black, you are to pour on the *Aqua Fortis* for an Hour or better at this laft Operation alone, that is, proportionably to the former. You may imagine, that no certain or general Rule can be given, either for the convenient Covering of the Places, or the exact Space of Time that is to be obferved in throwing on the Water: For it cannot be thought, that *Callot* pour'd as

E 3 much

much Water on his little Pieces, as he did on thofe which were bigger.

I have told you, how you may rub off your Varnifh or Ground, as Occafion requires, with a Charcoal, to fee whether the Water hath eat in deep enough : Then you will judge of the Space of Time, that you are to employ in pouring on the *Aqua Fortis*, by the various Works you are to do ; and where I tell you, that you may beftow an Hour and better on the laft Operation, my Meaning is, in Pieces that require much Blacknefs. Notwithftanding which, it is to be confidered, that all Copper, or all Sorts of *Aqua Fortis*, have not the fame Strength, Nature or Equality, therefore it muft be left to Difcretion.

Having, as before faid, poured the *Aqua Fortis* upon your Plate for an Hour, more or lefs, as the Work requires, wafh it again with fair Water, and dry it as in the preceding Operations ; then put it over the Fire, till your Mixture is all melted ; and wipe it very clean on both Sides, with a Linnen Cloth, till you have quite taken away all the Mixture.

S E C T.

S E C T. XVIII.

*To take the Ground or Varnish off the Plate,
after the* Aqua Fortis *has done its
Operation.*

TAKE Charcoal of Willow, or some
such soft-grain'd Wood, and after you
have taken off the Rind, and poured fair
Water on the Plate, rub it very even
with the Charcoal, as if you were to
polish Copper, and it will take off the
Varnish. Be careful that no Dust or Filth
fall upon the Plate ; and that the Charcoal
be free from Knots and Roughness, which
might occasion some small Scratches in the
Plate, and would be difficult to get out,
especially in those Places which are most
faint and sweet. Note, you are not to use
such a burnt Coal, as you do, to polish
withal.

When the Varnish is taken off, the
Plate is of an unpleasant Colour, by Reason
of the Operation of the Fire and Water
upon it. To reduce it therefore to its
proper Colour, take some ordinary *Aqua
Fortis*, to which add two third Parts of
fair Water, and with a little Linnen Rag
dipp'd therein, rub your Plate all over,

and you will find its Colour and Beauty return.

Then immediately take a dry Linnen Rag, and wipe it all over to take off all the aforefaid Water. Hold your Plate to the Fire, and pour on it a little Sallad-Oil, and with the Brims of an old Beaver roll'd up, rub your Plate all over with it, and with a Cloth wipe it dry.

This done, you will plainly perceive the Places, which require to be touched with the Graver, as for the moft Part it happens, efpecially in thofe Places, which are to be blackeft. For you may judge, that when there are many Strokes and Hatchings clofe to one another, there is fo little Varnifh between, that the *Aqua Fortis* commonly takes it off, and eats under it.

But if this happens, when you caft on your Water, you may prefently cover thofe Places, where you perceive the Varnifh break up, with the Mixture; it being more eafy to touch it afterwards with the Graver, than when the *Aqua Fortis* has made a Pit therein, which, in the Working it off at the Rolling-Prefs, caufes a large black Patch; but after fome Copies are taken off, that Patch becomes white, becaufe there is not any Thing for the Ink to faften on.

Having

Having covered that Part in Time, you have no more to do, but perfect thofe Strokes and Hatchings, to make them firm and beautiful; and then your Plate is ready for the Rolling-Prefs.

E 5   OF

O F
SOFT VARNISH.

✶✶✶✶✶✶✶✶✶✶✶✶✶✶✶✶✶✶✶✶

S E C T. XIX.

To make it, and its Uses.

TA K E two Ounces of Virgin Wax, half an Ounce of Burgundy Pitch, half an Ounce of common Pitch, put them into a clean and well-glaz'd earthen Pipkin, and when they are diffolved, take twoOunces of Afphaltum, let it be ground as fine as poffible, and fhake it into the Pipkin, and with a Stick keep ftirring it over the Fire, that the Afphaltum, and the reft, may incorporate well together, and be intirely diffolved, which will be done in about half a Quarter of an Hour; then take it off the Fire, and let it cool a little, and pour the faid Compofition into a Bafon of fair Water; your Hands being very clean, put them into it, and take out the faid Mixture before it be quite cold, and having well moulded it, and fqueezed out
the

the Water, roll it up into Pieces about an Inch Diameter, and two or three Inches long.

After it is moulded, wrap it up in a Piece of fine Sarfenet, or Taffata, two or three Times double, and so ufe it.

There are feveral other Compofitions of foft Varnifh, that may be ufed, but this I judge the beft of any I have met with.

Note, You are not to put in fo much Virgin Wax in Summer, as in Winter.

S E C T. XX.

The Manner of laying the foft Ground or Varnifh on the Plate.

HAVING your Plate well polifhed and cleanfed from Greafe, take the foft Varnifh prepared as is before mentioned, and put the faid Plate over a Chafing-difh, wherein a moderate Fire has been kindled, and let it be fo heated, that the Varnifh may eafily diffolve, as it paffes through the Sarfenet, in which 'tis wrapped. The Plate being thus heated, take the Varnifh cover'd as aforefaid, and by applying it to the End of the Roll, fpread it upon the Plate whilft it is hot, carrying it lightly from one Side

E 6   to

to the other, until the Plate be covered thin and equal all over : This being done, take some fine Sarsenet, or other fine Silk, doubled up, put some fine Cotton into it, and let it be about the Bigness of an Egg, when tied up, but make it broad at Bottom, then dab it gently all over your Plate, where you have laid the Varnish; taking Care it be not too thick, for when it is; your Work cannot be so fine and delicate as otherwise it would ; if the Plate should cool, and consequently the Varnish, you must heat it again, that it may receive the Varnish, as it passes through the Silk. Also take great Care, for your more easily spreading of it, that neither your Plate, nor Varnish burns ; which you will easily perceive, by observing, that when it is too hot, it casts itself into little Clots and Blisters.

As soon as you have spread your Varnish very even upon your Plate, black it over with the Flame of a Candle, after the same Manner I mentioned before in the hard Varnish ; taking Care that the Flame approach not too near ; this is to be done in one Case, rather than in another, that is, when having black'd it all over, you perceive, the Smoke hath not entered within the Varnish, by Reason of its growing
ing

ing cold : Therefore it will be convenient to put your Plate again over your Chafing-diſh, and you will ſee, as ſoon as the Plate is hot, the Varniſh will diſſolve; and thereby the Black, which the Smoke hath left upon the Varniſh, will pierce as far as the Plate.

In doing this, be very careful to have a moderate Fire, and continually remove your Plate, in ſuch a manner, that the Varniſh may melt equally all over it, without Burning.

After that, let your Plate cool, and when you think fit to work upon it, place your Deſign in the ſame Manner, as upon your hard Varniſh, (the Backſide thereof being rubb'd with the Duſt of Red Chalk, and Black Lead, mixed together) excepting only, that you muſt not lean ſo hard with your Point, in drawing the Out-lines of your Deſign, leſt by ſo do-ing, the Needle cutting through the Paper, ſhould rub the Varniſh.

Next you proceed to work upon your Plate, with the ſame kind of Points, as thoſe which are mentioned for hard Var-niſh, excepting the oval Points, which thoſe that etch with ſoft Varniſh never uſe: Neverthelefs they are very commo-dious, eſpecially for the working any Piece of Architecture, or making of large Strokes,

and

and 'tis left to the Choice of thofe that
grave, either to ufe them or not : But one
Thing is to be confidered, which you muft
be very careful of, and that is, how to keep
the foft Varnifh upon the Plate, for it is
very apt to be rubbed off, if any Thing
fhould happen to touch it. There are
feveral Ways of keeping it unhurt :
For Example, working upon the Plain,
or on a Defk, place on the Sides of
your Plate, two little Boards, of what
Thicknefs you pleafe, or two little Books
of the fame Thicknefs, and lay a thin Board
upon them, fo as not to touch the Plate,
and reft your Hand upon this Board as you
work.

Many work with their Plate laid upon an
Eafel, as a Painter does when he paints;
but all Men cannot fit in this Manner at
Work, although it is very much approved
of, for many Reafons, which hereafter fhall
be alledged.

To work upon the faid foft Varnifh,
you muft conveniently place your Board
upon a Defk, and lay a Piece of green
Bays upon that, and your Plate upon the
Bays. Afterwards, take a Linnen Cloth
without any kind of Seam, which has
been often put to other Ufes, that it may
be very foft. Then double it three or four
Times in Folds, and lay it upon your
Varnifh;

Varnifh; and reft your Hand on it, as you do on Sheets of Paper, upon hard Varnifh. The Reafon why this Caution is to be obferved is, left the Buttons of your Sleeve fhould rub off the Varnifh.

Be very careful, that there is no Duft or Filth upon your Varnifh; if you fee any upon your Plate, wipe it lightly off with one of your large foft Pencils, obferving, that much more Care is required for the preferving of foft Varnifh, than of hard; which made the Author leave it off, efpecially in Pieces that required long Time, and much Pains; it being much more eafy to make a firm Winding-Stroke upon hard Varnifh than upon foft; becaufe the Hardnefs of the Varnifh holds your Point, as it were engaged, which makes the Strokes the deeper, and more like the Firmnefs and Neatnefs of thofe of a Graver. Moreover, when you are at work on foft Varnifh, you muft have a fpecial Care, left any other Perfon than a Practitioner of the Art, touch or meddle with your Plate; and if any kind of greafy Matter happens to drop upon it, your Plate will be incurable: But if it happens to fall upon hard Varnifh, you may clean it with a Linnen Cloth, or Crumbs of Bread.

Thofe

Thofe that work upon foft Varnifh, if they put their Plate on a Defk or Eafel, are not in fo much Danger of rubbing off their Varnifh, nor need they fo often wipe away that which comes off in working; for the Plate being placed obliquely, the fuperfluous Matter falls away of itfelf. I don't think it neceffary to defcribe this Way of working, by a Plate, becaufe it is not probable that any who intend to etch after this Manner, can be ignorant how a Painter works upon an Eafel, there being no other Difference, except that a Painter ufes a Pencil, and a Graver his etching Tools. The Artift muft take Care to reft his Plate very firm, efpecially when he is very intent upon the making of any exact Strokes.

Callot worked upon hard Varnifh, after the fame Manner; but it was more to preferve his Health; fuppofing that to fit ftooping to his Work (though it were never fo little) would be hurtful to him.

S E C T. XXI.

To border the Plate, that it may contain the
Aqua Fortis.

GET foft Wax, either red or green; if it be in Winter, foften it in warm Water; in Summer it will be fufficiently
foft

foft of itfelf: In the managing of it, put
it round the Brims of your Plate, raifed
about half an Inch above the Surface of the
Plate, being, as it were, like a little Ram-
part or Wall, (forming at one Corner a
Spout to pour the *Aqua Fortis* off) in fuch
Sort, that placing your Plate very level,
and afterwards pouring your *Aqua Fortis*
upon it, the Water may be retained,
by Means of this Border of Wax,
and equally diffufed all over; but
before you pour it on (to prevent its
foaking through, between the Wax and the
Plate) dip your Pencil in your prepared
Tallow, and ftop the under Part neatly, on
the Infide of the Wax, fo that the *Aqua
Fortis* may not corrode under it.

· Having thus fecured your Plate, take
double *Aqua Fortis*, one Part, *Water*, two
Parts, mix them in a Glafs Bottle, or Stone
Mug; then pour it gently upon the
Plate, fo as that it may remain all
over it, the Thicknefs of half a Finger's
Breadth.

Then you will fee, that the Water will
work, and bubble up in thofe ftronger
Hatchings, that are moft firmly ftruck;
as for thofe that are fainter, you will perceive them clear at firft, and of the Colour
of the Copper, the Water not having, on
                              a fud-

a fudden, any other Effect than what appears to View.

Afterwards, when you have perceived the Water operate a fmall Time, pour it off from the Plate into fome Veffel, which is moft proper to contain it, as into an earthen Mug well glazed, or the like ; then throw fome fair Water upon the Plate, to extinguifh and wafh away the Remainder of the *Aqua Fortis*, which was upon it; then dry it by the Fire, as you have been taught before, when we difcourfed of hard Varnifh ; as to the foft Varnifh, and *Aqua Fortis* of the Refiners, be very careful to evaporate that Moifture, which, in the Winter Time, is commonly between the Copper and the Varnifh, before you lay on your *Aqua Fortis*; which being done, take your Mixture of Oil and Tallow, as is mentioned in the Beginning of this Difcourfe of hard Varnifh, and cover thofe Places with it, which ought to be moft tender and fweet ; or Picture Varnifh, mix'd with Lamp Black, as mentioned in the Operation of the hard Varnifh ; having covered them the firft Time, lay again upon your Plate the fame *Aqua Fortis* which you had taken away, and leave it on for half a Quarter of an Hour, or longer, according to your Difcretion ; then
take

take off the *Aqua Fortis*, and cover with your Mixture the next Places, as you fhall fee Occafion : And if you would have your Lines or Strokes be ftill deeper, then cover the fweeter Part by De-grees with your Mixture, that the *Aqua Fortis* may lie-the longer on the deeper Strokes.

Laftly, lay on the aforefaid *Aqua Fortis* again, and leave it on for the Space of half an Hour, or more, according to the Strength of the Water, and Nature of the Work; then take it away, and caft fome fair Water upon the Plate again.

This being done, take off your Border of Wax, and heat your Plate, fo that the oily Mixture, and Varnifh, may thorough-ly melt; then wipe it well with a Linnen Cloth, afterwards rub it all over with Olive Oil, and a Piece of old Beaver roll'd up, then touch it over again with your Graver, in thofe Places where it is necef-fary.

It is neceffary to obferve, that whilft the *Aqua Fortis* is upon your Plate, you muft take a Feather, and dip it to the Bot-tom of the faid *Aqua Fortis*, fweeping it along, to remove the Froth or Scum, which gathers upon your Strokes or Hatchings, whilft the Water performs its Operation; as alfo, to give the more Way to the Operation

tion of the Water, and fee if the Varnifh be not broke up, which the Bubbling of the Water hinders you from difcerning.

Take Notice alfo, that the *Aqua Fortis* of the hard Varnifh, will ferve excellently well, to eat into the Work made by the aforefaid foft Varnifh, and that the Manner of applying the oily Mixture, is the fame with that of hard Varnifh, and whoever ufes it may be affured, that it is much better for this Purpofe, than that of the Refiners : Moreover, it is not fo fubject to caufe the Varnifh to break up, nor to many other Accidents ; as being hurtful to the Sight, and Health, as that of the Refiners is ; neverthelefs, let every one make ufe of which Sort he pleafes.

SECT. XXII.

The Manner of laying a white Ground upon the hard or foft Varnifh.

THERE is a Way to whiten your Varnifhes upon the Plate, inftead of making them black with a Candle, which is thus.

When you have applied your hard Varnifh (as has been obferved) upon the Plate, harden it over the Fire, without blacking it, yet in the fame Manner as if

it

it were blacked, then let the Plate cool, and having got white Cerus, put it into an earthen Difh well leaded, and a little Flanders Starch, fet them over a Fire, and melt them together, making them pretty hot; that being done, take up the white Cerus, (which ought to be pretty clear) with a Brufh, or great Pencil of Hog's Hair, and whiten your Varnifh with it, laying it as thin and even as you can, then leave it to dry, laying the Plate flat, in fome convenient Place; if by Chance in whitening it, the White be difficult to fpread, you need only put among the faid white Cerus a Drop or two of the Gall of an Ox, and mix them together in the Difh with your Brufh. For the foft Var-nifh, you may do the fame, after you have laid it upon your Plate, and extended it very even with the feathered End of your Quills: Some will fay, if they black the Plate, before the White is put upon it, when they come to grave, the Hatchings will be the more black, and confequently will appear fo much the more diftinct to the Eye. But to this I an-fwer;

First, When the Plate is blacked, the White will not touch it, nor muft they ven-ture to put fo much Gall, for Fear of fpoiling the Varnifh.

Secondly,

Secondly, If the White fhould fpread well, it will not appear otherwife than grey, by Reafon of the blacking of the faid Varnifh, unlefs you lay it fo thick, as to fpoil the whole Work.

The marking of your Defign upon foft Varnifh, is performed with the Duft of red Chalk, (as before mentioned of hard Varnifh) or by rubbing the Paper well, or Defign, with the Duft of black Chalk, or black Lead, when the Varnifh is made white : For red Chalk is moft proper for a black Ground.

When you have graved what you intend upon the foft Varnifh, and are going to etch your Plate with *Aqua Fortis*; what you have then to do, is to take a little fair Water, fomething more than lukewarm, and caft it upon the faid Plate : then with a foft clean Spunge, or Duck's Wing-Feathers, moiften the faid white Cerus all over with it; afterwards wafh the Plate, to take off the Whiting, and dry it.

Laftly, you may lay on which of the two Sorts of *Aqua Fortis* you pleafe; and for the preferving of the faid white Varnifh, whilft you are working, you need only lay upon it a Piece of foft Linnen, or Damafk Linnen, inftead of Paper.

If

If you choofe rather to take away the faid Whiting, you muft take fome *Aqua Fortis* of the Refiners, tempered with fair Water, lay it upon the Plate, difperfing it all over, which will foak and quickly eat in; after you have thrown clean fair Water upon it to take away the Whiting, let the Water dry up, which remains upon the Plate, and caufes it to eat into your Work, as I faid before.

SECT. XXIII.

Another Way to lay a White on the Varnifh.

TAKE the beft Cerus, and grind it very fine upon a Stone, with fair Water, which being done, take Gum-Water, and pour a fmall Quantity of it upon the Stone, and mix it with the Cerus; then take a large Pencil of Camel's Hair, and with that Pencil take it off the Stone, and fpread it thin all over your Plate; and immediately after, take a larger Pencil of Camel's Hair, and with a very light and gentle Hand, pafs it all over the Plate, fo as to make it lie exactly even in all Parts, that the Strokes of the former Brufh, may not appear, then lay your Plate very even, and let it dry.

If

It will be neceffary to give you this Notice, that you are not to mix too much Gum with the White, nor too little; for if there be too much, it will break and crack the Varnifh; if there be too little, it will eafily rub off: Therefore you muft be careful to ufe no more, than will juft ferve to bind the White upon the Plate. Like-wife you muft have a care not to lay it too thick, for if it be, you cannot work with the Neatnefs and Curioufnefs, you may otherwife.

S E C T. XXIV.

The Manner, after the Plates are eat in by the Aqua Fortis, *to touch or re-grave that which you have forgot, or which you would mend or fupply.*

BEFORE I make an End, it is pro-per to fhew you the Manner how to retouch many Things, according as Need may require, by the Means of *Aqua Fortis*; if it happens that you have made upon your Copper, any thing that does not pleafe you, and for this Caufe having covered it with your oily Mixture, that the *Aqua Fortis* fhould not perform its Operation, or that you would add any Ornaments,

either

either in Drapery, or any other thing which may be thought on: In this Cafe, take your Plate, and rub it well over with Olive Oil in thofe Places, where there is any thing graven, in fuch Manner that the Blacknefs and Foulnefs, which is like to be in the Hatchings or Strokes, may be taken away. Afterwards take out the Greafe fo thoroughly with Crumbs of Bread, that there may remain none, nor Filth upon the Plate, or in any of the Strokes or Hatchings.

Then heat it over a Charcoal Fire, and fpread the foft Varnifh upon it, as has been faid before. What you are to take fpecial Care of, is, that the Hatchings, which you would have remain, be filled with Varnifh; which being done, black it, and then you may retouch, or add what you intend. Laftly, make your Hatchings with your Needles, according as the Manner of the Work fhall require, being careful, before you put on the *Aqua Fortis*, to cover with your oily Mixture (as is faid before) the firft graving which was upon your Plate; for if the Varnifh fhould not have entred all over, that certainly will: Infomuch that, if there fhould happen in fome Places of the Hatchings to be neither Mixture,

F　　　　　　nor

nor Varnish, the *Aqua Fortis* will not fail
to enter and spoil all. Having caused
the *Aqua Fortis* to eat into your Work,
take away your Varnish from your Plate,
by the Means of Fire, as before said.

T H E

THE
ART
OF
ENGRAVING.

SECT. XXV.

The several Ways of drawing the Design upon the Plate.

BEFORE I fpeak of the Manner of managing and whetting your Graver, I think it will not be amifs to let you know the Ways that are ufed in drawing your Defign upon the Plate; which mutt be of the fame Bignefs the Defign or Print is, which you intend to copy.

Put your Plate over the Fire, and let it heat a little; then take a Piece of the whiteft Virgin Wax, and fpread it thin over the Plate, and with a fmooth Feather gently ftroke it all over, fo that it may lie very even and fmooth; then let it cool. If you intend to copy a Print, and would have it to print off the fame Way when it is graved, with your Print; then you muſt place your Print which you would grave, with the Face or printed Side next to your Plate, waxed over as before mentioned; and having placed it very true, rub the Backſide of the Print with a Burniſher (or any Thing that is ſmooth and round) and you will find, that it will ſtick to the Wax which is upon the Copper: When you have ſo done, take off the Print, beginning at one Side or Corner, but be careful you take it not off too haſtily, for by ſo doing, you may tear your Print or Deſign; and alſo, if you put your Wax too thick upon the Plate, it will be a Means to cauſe the ſame Inconvenience.

But if you would grave it the ſame Way, as your Print or Deſign is, then take the Duſt of black Lead, or black Chalk, and rub the Backſide of your Drawing or Print all over therewith, and place it with that Side blacked towards the Plate ſo waxed, (as before mentioned) and with your Needle, or Drawing Point, draw all the Out-lines of your Deſign, and you will find all thoſe Lines upon your Plate ; but if you deſire to preſerve the Backſide of your Deſign from being blacked with
the

the Duſt aforeſaid ; then take a fine thin
Piece of white Paper of the Bigneſs of your
Deſign, and inſtead of rubbing the Backſide of your Print or Deſign, rub one
Side of the ſaid Paper with the Duſt or
Powder of black Chalk, and placing it
with the Side ſo blacked, next to the
waxed Plate, lay the Backſide of your
Deſign upon the Paper, and fix them
both firm to your Plate at each Corner with
a little Wax, then draw the Out-lines of
your Deſign : only note, that you muſt
lean ſomewhat harder with your Needle in
Drawing.

There are other Ways uſed for this
Purpoſe, which it is needleſs to trouble you
with ; only take Notice, that in Caſe you
deſire to preſerve your Deſign from being
any Way defaced by the Marks of your
Needle in drawing the Out-lines, take a
fine Piece of white Paper, and having oil'd
it, hold it by the Fire, ſo that the Oil may
ſooner penetrate it ; and having ſo done,
wipe it very dry with a Linnen Rag, and
place the ſaid Paper upon your Deſign,
making it faſt at each Corner, and you
will perfectly diſcern your Deſign through
the Paper ; then with a black Lead well
pointed, draw all the Out-lines of your
Deſign upon the ſaid oiled Paper, which

F 3 done,

done, place it upon the Plate in the fame
Manner as before.

S E C T. XXVI.

*The Forms of Graving-Tools, and the Manner
of whetting the Graver.*   Pl. 9.

THE upper Part of this Figure will
fhew two Sorts of Graving-Tools,
the one formed Square, the other Lozenge :
The Square Graver makes a broad and
fhallow Stroke, or Hatch; and the Lozenge makes a deep and narrower Stroke.
The Ufe of the Square Graver, is to make
the largeft Strokes; and the Ufe of the
other, is to make the more delicate and
lively Strokes.   But a Graver made of an
indifferent Size between thefe two is beft,
and will make your Strokes, or Hatches,
fhew with more Life and Vigour ; and
yet with fufficient Force, if you manage
it properly in your working.   The Forms
of thefe Gravers, you will fee in the Figures
I. and II.

The IIId Figure fhews you how to
whet the two Sides of your Graver, which
is to be done in the following Manner;
you muft have a very good Oil-ftone
fmooth and flat, and having poured a little
Sallad Oil thereupon, take the Graver,
and

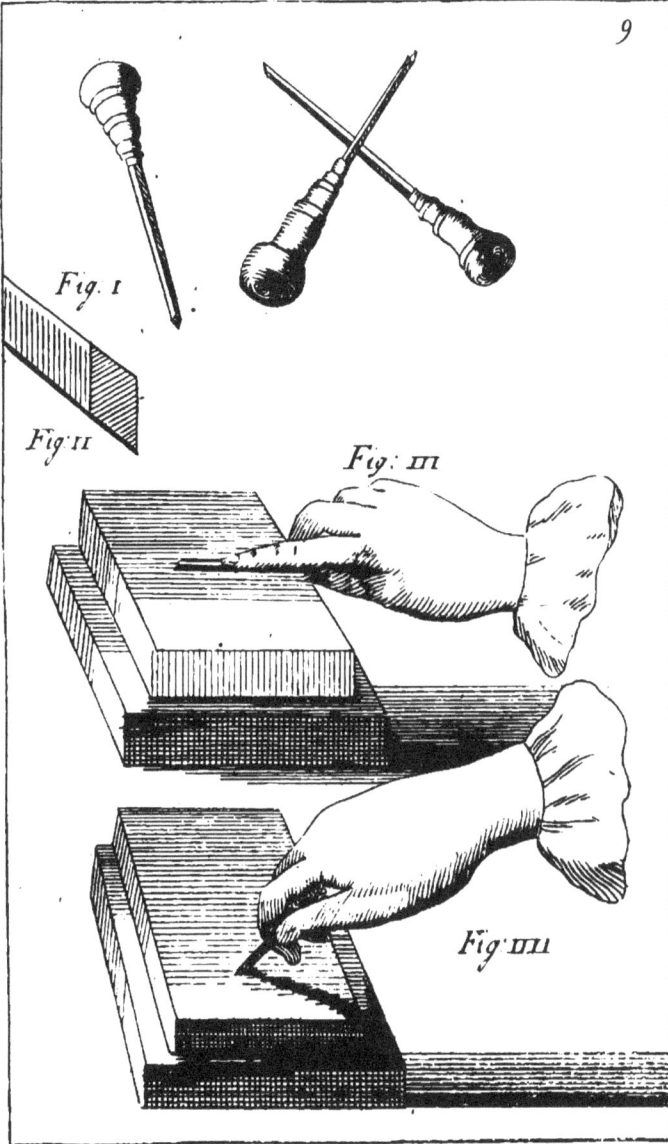

Fig. 1

Fig. II

Fig. III

Fig. IIII

and laying that Side of it which you intend ſhall cut the Copper, flat upon the Stone, whet it very flat and even ; and in doing this, take particular Care to place your Fore-finger very firmly upon the oppoſite Side of your Graver ; that you may carry your Hand ſteadily, preſs equally on it, and guide it with the more Exactneſs : Then turn the next Side of your Graver, and whet that as you did the other ; that there may be a very ſharp Edge for the Space of an Inch or better ; then turning uppermoſt that Edge which you have ſo whetted, and ſetting the End of your Graver obliquely upon the Stone, carry your Hand exactly even, to the End that it may be whetted very flat and ſloping, in the Form of a Lozenge, making a ſharp Point to the Edge, as Figure IIII. ſhews you.

It is abſolutely neceſſary, to be very exact in the Whetting of your Graver ; for it is impoſſible you ſhould ever work with the Neatneſs and Curioſity you deſire, if your Graver be not very good, and rightly whetted.

SECT. XXVII.

The Manner of holding the Graver, with other Particulars.

Y O U may fee alfo, that the uppermoft Part of this Figure defcribes the Form of two Gravers to you, with their Handles fitted for Whetting. They that ufe this Art, before they ufe them, commonly cut away that Part of the Knob or Bowl which is at the End of their Handles, and upon the fame Line with the Edge of their Graver; that it may not obftruct or hinder them in their Graving, as Figure II. fhews you.

For if you work upon a large Plate, you will find that Part of your Handle (if it be not cut away) will reft fo upon the Copper, that it will hinder the fmooth and even Carriage of your Hand in making your Strokes or Hatches; and will alfo make your Graver run into the Copper in fuch a manner, that you will not be able to manage it as you would.

The third Figure defcribes the Way of holding your Graver; which is in this Manner. You muft place the Knob or Ball of the Handle of your Graver in

the

2

1

Fig: II

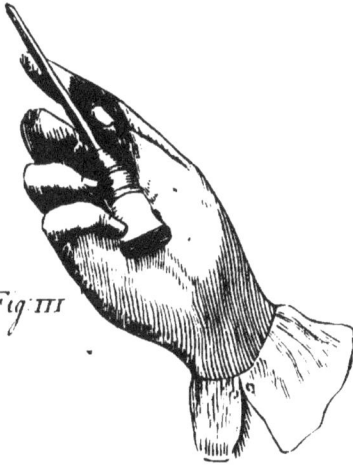

Fig. III

the Hollow of your Hand, and having extended your Fore-finger towards the Point
of your Graver, laying it oppofite to the
Edge that fhould cut the Copper, place
your other Fingers on the Side of your
Handle, and your Thumb on the other
Side of the Graver, fo that you may guide
your Graver flat and parallel with the
Plate ; as you may fee in Figure IIII.

Be careful that your Fingers do not in-
terpofe between the Plate and the Graver,
for they will be troublefome, and hinder
you in carrying your Graver level with the
Plate, fo that you cannot make your
Strokes with that Freedom and Neatnefs
you otherwife may. This I think fit to
give you Notice of in this Place, becaufe
you muft firft learn to hold your Graver
perfectly well, and be able to practife without Pain or Difficulty ; or elfe you will
not acquire that Readinefs and Command
of Hand, which is required in an accurate
and fkilful Engraver.

S E C T. XXVIII.

The Manner of governing the Hand in Graving, and other Particulars.

HAVING defcribed the Way of holding your Graver, the next Thing is to fhew you how to guide it upon the Plate, in making of your Strokes, either ftraight or crooked. To work with the more Eafe and Convenience, you muft have a ftrong round Leather Cufhion filled with Sand, or fine Duft; let it be made about half a Foot broad in the Diameter, and three or four Inches deep; lay this upon a Table which ftands faft and firm; then lay your Plate upon the Cufhion, as is feen in Figure II. in the former Section.

When you make any ftraight Strokes, hold your Graver as directed before; and when your Strokes are to be deeper or broader in one Place than in another, where you would have them deepeft, you muft prefs your Hand hardeft; but in making of a ftraight Stroke, be very careful to hold your Plate firmly upon the Cufhion.

When you make any crooked or winding Strokes, hold your Hand and

Graver

Graver fteadily, and as you work, turn your Plate againft your Graver; otherwife it will be impoffible, for you to make any crooked or winding Strokes with that Neatnefs and Command of Hand, you by this Means may.

If, when you are working, your **Graver** happens to break the Point often, it is too hard tempered; to cure which, take a red hot Charcoal, and lay the End of your Graver upon it, and when you perceive it grow yellowifh, dip it in Tallow : If your Graver become blunt without breaking, it is worth nothing.

It will be convenient for you to have a Piece of Box, or hard Wood, to ftrike the Point of your Graver into, after you have fharpened it; which will take off all the Roughnefs about the Point, that was caufed by whetting it upon the Oil-ftone. After you have graved Part of your Work, it will be neceffary to fcrape the Plate with the fharp Edge of another Graver, carrying it even upon it, to take off the Roughnefs of the Strokes; but in fo doing, take heed not to make any new Scratches in your Work.

That you may the better fee what is graved, roll up clofe a Piece of black Felt or Caftor, liquored over a

little

little with Olive Oil, and rub the graved
Places with it : If you perceive any
Scratches in your Plate, rub them out with
your Burniſher; and if you have graved
any of your Strokes too deep, you may
make them appear fainter by rubbing them
with the ſame.

MEZZOTINTO,

MEZZOTINTO, *called Scraping or Burniſh-ing on Copper.*

TAKE a well poliſhed Copper Plate, and make it all over rough one Way, with a particular Engine deſigned for that Purpoſe, then croſs it over again with the ſame Engine, and if there is Oc-caſion, croſs it over a third Time; till it be made rough all over alike.

When you have thus roughed the Plate, then rub Charcoal, black Chalk, or black Lead over the Plate, and draw your Deſign with white Chalk on it; then take a Tracer, made of the Point of a Needle, blunted round, ſtuck at the End of a Piece of Cane, and trace out the Out-lines of the Deſign, which you drew with the white Chalk: And where you would have the Light ſtrike the ſtrongeſt, take a Burniſher, or Scraper, and burniſh that Part of the Plate as clean and ſmooth as it was, when the Plate was firſt poliſhed.

Where you would have the Light fainter, there you muſt not poliſh it ſo much; and after this Manner you muſt either increaſe or diminiſh the Light in your Deſign, by mak-ing it fainter or ſtronger, as the Neceſſity of the Work requires.

An

An IDEA *of a fine* COLLECTION *of* PRINTS.

THIS Collection, which will be very numerous, may be divided into three principal Parts; the *First*, to contain all *Historical Subjects*; the *Second*, all the *Subjects of Morality*; and the *Third*, every Thing that concerns the *Progress of the Arts of Painting*, *Sculpture* and *Engraving*; to which may be added a *Fourth*, containing *mixed Subjects*.

The *Historical Subjects* will contain the *History of the World*, according to its different *Ages*, *Monarchies* and *Nations*; represented by many Maps, Battle-Pieces, Medals, Statues, Bafs-Reliefs, Portraits and Buildings, Atchievements and Seals, Devices, Tombs, and other Monuments of illuftrious Perfons.

The *Moral Subjects* will contain a great Number of Emblems, Enigmas and Devices, concerning the Religion, Manners and Politicks of different Nations, with Reprefentations of the Virtues and Vices.

The *Subjects* of the *Progress of the Arts*, will contain the different *Stiles* of the Arts; by comparing the antique Remains and Ruins of them, with the Works of the
Gothick

Gothick Ages, and of thofe Mafters who have flourifhed within thefe 250 Years; in order, by that Means, to obferve their Original, Increafe and Decay; and laftly, their Re-eftablifhment in the Perfection and Beauty we now fee them.

The *mixed Subjects* may contain Volumes of Portraits of eminent Women, Hunting-Pieces, various comical and grotefque Subjects, &c.

But as thefe three different Sorts of Subjects deferve a more accurate Defcription, that the Curious may fee what each Volume ought to contain, in order to form a more agreeable Symmetry between them; I will give an exact Account what each Volume fhould be compofed of.

The firft fhould contain what paffed in the Beginning of the World, according to the Books of *Mofes, Genefis, Exodus, Leviticus, Numbers,* and *Deuteronomy.*

The 2d ought to be a Sequel of the Sacred Hiftory, as it is found in the Books of *Jofhua, Judges, Ruth,* and *Kings.*

The 3d fhould contain the Remainder of the Hiftory of the Old Teftament, according to the Books of *Efdras, Tobit, Judith, Efther, Job,* the *Prophets,* and the *Maccabees.*

The 4th may fhew us an Abridgment of Nature, the Compofition of the World, according

according to the Poets and ancient Heathen Philofophers; the four Elements; the Heavens, the Conftellations, Planets, and fixed Stars; the Fire; the Air, Winds, and Birds; the Water; the Seas, Rivers, and Fifh; the Earth, its ancient Geography; fome uncommon Trees, Flowers, and other Curiofities of Nature; Time, the Hours, the Months, and Seafons; the fabulous People and Animals; Man, his Creation and Compofition, his different Ages, Manners, and Senfes; his Wonders, and Inventions in the Liberal and Mechanick Arts.

The 5th fhould contain the fabulous Hiftory of the Ancients, of *Saturn* and *Cybele*, of *Jupiter* and *Juno*, of *Neptune* and *Amphitrite*, of *Galatea*, and many other aquatick and marine Deities; of *Pluto* and *Proferpine*, of the infernal Deities and Torments; of *Apollo* and *Diana*; which may be confirmed by their different Medals and Statues.

The 6th, what may ferve to illuftrate the fabulous Hiftory of *Mars*, of *Vulcan* and *Venus*, of *Cupid* and *Pfyche*, of *Minerva* and the *Mufes*, of *Mercury*, *Bacchus*, and *Hercules*.

The 7th, a Series of the Hiftory of the Gods, where there will be fome Fables, Medals and Statues of the Demi-Deities, whofe

whofe Names, becaufe of their great Number, I fhall omit.

The 8th may contain the Hiftory of what is called the *Heroick Times*, the Voyage of the *Argonauts*, the War of *Thebes*, and alfo *Ovid*'s Metamorphofes.

The 9th fhould fhew the War of *Troy*, the Voyages of *Æneas* and *Ulyffes*, with the laft Acts of the Heroick Ages.

In the 10th, there may be fome Subjects of the *Grecian* Hiftory; the Medals, Portraits, and Statues of their illuftrious Men; with fome Pieces relating to *Sicily*, and that Part of *Italy*, which was anciently called the *Greater Greece*.

The 11th fhould contain fome Maps and Actions of the firft and fecond Monarchies of the *Affyrians* and *Perfians*; with fome other *Afiatick*, *Ægyptian*, and *African* Hiftories.

The 12th, the third Monarchy of the *Macedonians*, comprehending the Acts of *Alexander* the *Great*, and his Succeffors.

The 13th the Commencement of the fourth Monarchy of the *Romans*; the Reigns of their feven Kings; under *Numa Pompilius* may be ranged all thofe Pieces, which relate to the Religion, Sacrifices, Ceremonies, and Burials of the *Romans*; under *Tullus Hoftilius*, every Thing that relates to their Militia; and under *Tarquinius Prifcus*,

Priscus, whatever can give us an Idea of their Habits, Ornaments, Magnificence, and Triumphs, with the Pomp of their publick Spectacles, Feasts, and Baths.

The 14th may contain Part of the Transactions of the *Roman* Republick, from the Expulsion of their Kings, under their Consuls and Dictators, 'till the Time of *Julius Cæsar*; and to make this Volume compleat, there should be a Collection of Medals, and other Monuments of the ancient *Roman* Families.

The 15th, what we have of the Reigns of their Emperors, *Julius Cæsar*, and *Augustus*.

In the 16th, we may see the Manner of making War, of the *Greeks*, *Romans*, and ancient Barbarians. We may here have several Plans of the Marches of Armies, Prospects of Camps, of Battles, and the Sieges of Cities, purposely omitted in the preceding Volumes, to assemble them here together, in order to give us an Idea of the ancient Manner of making War; and at the End of this Volume, there should be a Collection of all Sorts of Shipping, ancient and modern.

The 17th will shew us the Subjects of the Birth, Life, and Miracles of our Saviour, who was born in the 42d Year of the *Roman* Empire, under the Reign of *Augustus*;

Auguſtus; where the Chriſtian Æra begins.

The 18th may contain the Death and
Sufferings of our Lord and Saviour; and
a Collection of Holy Parables.

The 19th, the Reigns of the Emperors
Tiberius, Caligula, and *Claudius*; under
which will be contained the Hiſtory of the
Infant Chriſtian Church.

The 20th, what paſſed under *Nero* and
his Succeſſors, to the End of the Reign of
Trajan; and this with Regard to both ſa-
cred and prophane Hiſtory.

The 21ſt, the Hiſtory of the *Dacian*
War, as it is repreſented in the Column of
Trajan.

The 22d ſhould comprehend the Ages,
and Reigns of the Emperors, from *Adrian*,
to the Government of *Alexander*, the Son
of *Mammæa.*

The 23d, the Emperors from *Alexander*,
to the Time of *Conſtantine* the *Great.*

The 24th, the Empire of *Conſtantine*
and his Children, to the End of *Theoda-
fius*'s Reign, which may be called the laſt
Period of the *Roman* Grandeur; and at the
End of this Volume ſhould be placed
the Eccleſiaſtical Geography of the Patri-
archates.

The 25th ſhould contain the Diſſipation
and Diviſion of the *Roman* Empire, which
began

began to be ufurped by the barbarous Nations, in the Times of *Arcadius* and *Honorius*, and ended in the *Eaft*, by the taking of *Conftantinople*, in the Year 1453.

The 26th, the difmal Conclufion of the Eaftern Affairs in *Afia*, by the Conquefts of *Mahomet*, and other *Ottoman* Emperors, by the Sophies of *Perfia*, and the Kams of *Tartary*.

The 27th fhould be a Series of the *Mahometan* Princes, and *Ægyptian* Sultans; the Cheriffs of *Morocco*, and Kings of *Barbary*, that have reigned in *Africa*; and afterwards there fhould be a Collection of Hiftorical Pieces relating to this third Part of the Globe; the *Abyffins*, the Kingdoms of *Congo*, and feveral others.

The 28th fhould contain the Habits and Ornaments of the Chriftian *Greeks*, and other Subjects of the Grand Segnior; with thofe of the *Turks* and *Perfians*; of the *Tartars*, and other barbarous Nations; and at the End fhould be a Collection of fome Cruelties, Executions, and Punifhments.

The 29th fhould be the Commencement of the Religious Orders, which were inftituted in the *Eaft*; and amongft others, of the Orders of St. *Anthony*, St. *Bafil*, the *Crofs-Bearers*, the *Jeromites*, and the *Carmelites*.

The

The 30th, fome Hiftorical Pieces of the Knights of *Malta,* who were alfo inftituted in the *Eaft,* under the Name of *Knights Hofpitallers of St. John of Jerufalem.*

The 31ft fhould contain the Inftitution of the *Weftern* Religious Orders, and particularly of thofe of St. *Auguftin,* and St. *Bennet.*

The 32d, the different Orders that have flourifhed in the *Eaft,* fince St. *Bennet,* to the Time of St. *Dominick,* and St. *Francis;* that is to fay, of the *Carthufians, Premon-ftratenfes,* of the *Shady-Valley,* the *Mathu-rins,* and of the Order of the *Ciftercians.*

The 33d fhould contain the Order of the *Dominicans,* and fome Hiftorical Pieces of the *Holy Rofary;* and afterwards a Collection of the Images of the Virgin *Mary,* which are held in Veneration by moft *Roman Catholicks.*

The 34th, whatever can give us an Idea of the Life of St. *Francis,* and of the moft remarkable male and female Saints of his three Orders; and laftly, there fhould be a Defcription of his Defert of *Averne.*

The 35th fhould be the Sequel of the Order of Saint *Francis,* containing fome Pieces relating to the Order of the *Capuchins.*

The 36th fhould contain whatever there is relating to the Orders and Religious Confraternities

Confraternities that have arifen in the Church of *Rome*, fince St. *Francis* and St. *Dominick*, to this prefent Time.

In the 37th there fhould be a Collection of all the Habits and Ornaments of Ecclefiaftical Perfons, and of all the Orders of Monks and Nuns.

The 38th. fhould be filled with the Reprefentations of Religious Ceremonies, and of the Magnificence of the Court of *Rome*.

The 39th, with the Ceremonies and Pomps practifed at the Interments of Chriftians, and of the ancient Pagans, and barbarous Nations.

The 40th and 41ft fhould contain various publick Rejoicings, and Entries, Triumphs, Tournaments, Fireworks, Comedies, Dances and Mafquerades.

The 42d, the Chronological Hiftory of the Papacy, divided into Centuries, from the Time of Pope *Leo* the IIId, to whom *Charles* the *Great* gave the City of *Rome*, to the prefent Pontificate.

The 43d, the Sequel of the Hiftory of the *Weft*, containing a particular Defcription of the modern City of *Rome*, its Churches, Palaces, publick Buildings, Villas, Ornaments, and the remaining Monuments of its ancient Grandeur.

The

The 44th, Hiftorical Subjects relating to *Italy* in particular; and firft of the Temporal State of the *Pope*, as it is now-a-days, both within, and out of *Italy*.

The 45th fhould contain the Sovereign States of *Italy*; and in this Volume there fhould be a Collection of what relates to the Republicks of *Venice*, *Genoa*, *Lucca*, *Ragufa*, and *St. Marino*.

The 46th, the Sequel of *Italy*, containing the Dominions of the Kings of the *Sicilies*, and *Sardinia*, the *Grand Duke* of *Tufcany*, Duke of *Modena*, and of the Houfe of *Auftria*, and other Princes in *Italy*.

The 47th, the Hiftorical Subjects relating to the Kingdoms and States of the King of *Spain*, in *Old Spain*.

The 48th, thofe of the Kingdom of *Portugal*; and afterwards thofe concerning the Defcription of both *Spains*.

The 49th fhould be a Collection of Hiftorical Pieces, relating to the Dominions of the Houfe of *Auftria*, in the *Low Countries*.

The 50th, a Collection of thofe relating to the Dominions of the King of *Spain* in the *New World*; and here fhould be every Thing that regards *America*.

The 51ft, the Dominions of the King of *Spain* in *Afia*; under which fhould be
comprifed

comprifed what relates to the *Eaft-Indies*, *China*, *Japan*, *India Proper*, and the reft of the *Indian* Princes.

The 52d fhould be a Collection of what concerns the Republick of the *United Provinces*.

The 53d, an Hiftorical Collection of whatever regards the Kingdoms of *England* and *Ireland*, to the End of the Reign of Queen *Elizabeth*.

The 54th, of what relates to the Kingdom of *Scotland*; and to the three Kingdoms of *England*, *Scotland*, and *Ireland*, fince the Union of thofe Crowns in the Perfon of King *James* the VIth of *Scotland*, and Ift of *England*; with a Defcription of this Monarchy.

The 55th, of what regards the *Northern* States; that is to fay, *Ruffia*, *Poland*, *Sweden*, *Denmark*, and other *Northern* Countries.

The 56th fhould contain the States of the Kingdoms of *Bohemia*, and *Hungary*, the Arch-Dutchy of *Auftria*, the County of *Tirol*, and other hereditary Dominions of the Houfe of *Auftria*.

The 57th, the Hiftorical Subjects concerning the Emperors of *Germany*, from *Conrad*, Duke of *Franconia*, who tranf- ferred the Empire from the *French* to the *Germans*, to the late Emperor.

The

The 58th, what relates to the nine Electors of the Empire, as well the Ecclefiaftical as the Secular.

The 59th, what relates to the other *German* Princes, both Ecclefiaftical and Secular.

The 60th, what regards the Free Cities of the Empire.

The 61ft fhould cóntain whatever relates to the Republicks of *Switzerland*, *Geneva*, the *Grifons*, the Principality of *Neufchatel*, and the other Allies and Subjects of the *Switzers*.

The 62d, what concerns the Dutchies of *Burgundy*, *Normandy*, *Lorrain*, and *Britany*, before they were united to the *French* Monarchy.

The 63d fhould contain the Antiquities of the *Gauls*, and the Portraits of their illuftrious Men, before the coming of the *Franks*, under their firft King *Pharamond*.

The 64th, what regards the Hiftory of the *French*, during the firft Race of their Kings, after their Arrival in *Gaul*, under the Conduct of *Pharamond*.

The 65th, what regards the fecond Race of their Kings, from *Pepin*, to *Louis* the Vth.

The 66th fhould begin with the third Race of their Kings, and contain every Thing that relates to them, from *Hugh*

Capet, to the End of the Reign of *Charles* the *Fair* ; where the Right Line of the eldeft Branch ended.

The 67th fhould contain what concerns their Kings of the third Race, from *Philip* of *Valois*, to the Death of *Louis* XI.

The 68th, the Reigns of their Kings, *Charles* the VIII. *Louis* the XII. *Francis* the I. and *Henry* the II. ; and as by the Marriage of *Mary* of *Burgundy*, with *Maximilian*, *Europe* has been fince divided into the two Families of *Auftria* and *Bourbon* ; to avoid Confufion, thofe Pieces relating to the foreign Wars of the *French*, with the Portraits of the eminent Men, who have been either their Allies or Enemies, may be put under the Reigns of their Kings.

The 69th and 70th may contain the Reigns of their Kings, *Francis* the II. *Charles* the IX. and *Henry* the III.

The 71ft, what relates to the Order of the *Holy Ghoft*, which was inftituted by *Henry* the III. and here may be the Names and Arms of all the Commanders and Knights of the Order, from its firft Inftitution to the laft Creation.

The 72d, what relates to the Reign of *Henry* the IV.

The 73d may contain the Beginning of the Reign of *Louis* the XIII. his Portraits, thofe

thofe of the Queen, the Princes and Prin-
ceffes of the Blood ; with the Arms or
Portraits of the Cardinals, Bifhops, and
great Officers of the Crown, and Houfe-
hold.

The 74th, the Arms and Portraits of
fome Ecclefiafticks, Religious, and Secu-
lars, of all Conditions, who lived, and
were engraved, during the Reign of *Louis*
the XIII. to which may alfo be joined *Van-
Dyk*'s Portraits.

The 75th, fome Pieces of the magnifi-
cent Ceremonies, Rejoicings, and other
Feftivals, that paffed in *France*, in the
Reign of *Louis* the XIII.

The 76th, what paffed of the fame Kind
in Foreign Countries, during this Reign.

The 77th, the Pieces reprefenting the
warlike Exploits of the *French* Nation,
from the Beginning of the Reign of *Louis*
the XIII. to the Year 1629 ; when all the
cautionary Towns of the Proteftants were
reduced to his Obedience.

The 78th, the military Actions that
paffed in *Europe*, from the Time of *Louis*
the XIII. to the Rupture of the Peace with
Spain, in the Year 1635.

The 79th, the military Actions, from
the Treaty of Peace at *Treves*, to the Death
of *Louis* the XIII.

The

The 80th may contain the Habits and Ornaments of the ancient and modern *French*, from the firſt Eſtabliſhment of that Monarchy, to the preſent Time ; to which may be added, thoſe of the conquered Provinces, with the Cries of *Paris*, *Callot*'s Beggars, and the Country Sports and Paſtimes of the *French*.

The 81ſt, a Series of the military Actions during the Reign of *Louis* the XIV. the Regency of the Duke of *Orleans*, and the Reign of *Louis* the XV. now living.

The 82d, a Series of the magnificent Ceremonies, Feſtivals, publick Rejoicings, Fireworks, *&c.* during the ſame Time.

The 83d ſhould be a Geographical Deſcription of the *French* Monarchy, as it is now divided into Provinces, Parliaments, Governments, Generalities, Dioceſes, and Sub-diviſions; to which ſhould be added, Charts of the Coaſts, Plans, or Profils of the fortified Towns and Fortreſſes, of the principal Churches, and publick Buildings, and of the Royal Palaces, with thoſe of the Princes of the Blood, Nobility, and Gentry.

The 84th ſhould contain Maps of the States and Provinces, with Plans or Profils of the principal Towns and Fortreſſes, which have been added to the *French* Monarchy,

narchy, from the Beginning of the Reign of *Louis* the XIII. to the prefent Time.

The 85th, the Portraits of all the eminent Men in the Kingdom of *France*, either for Arts or Arms, fince the Reign of *Louis* the XIII. to the prefent Time ; to which may be added, thofe of *Flanders*, and other Countries.

The 86th may be compofed of the Portraits of thofe People, who ought to be avoided ; fuch as, the Authors of different Sects, of Men noted for Impiety or *Libertinifm*, &c. to which may be added the Reprefentations of Monfters.

The 87th may be compofed of the Portraits of Saints and Martyrs, and thofe of their Perfecutors, with Reprefentations of the various Tortures that have been inflicted on them, from the Beginning of the World to this Time.

The Pieces which will illuftrate the Arts of *Painting*, *Sculpture*, and *Engraving*, will alfo compofe many Volumes.

The 1ft of which may contain the Original of the Art of Painting, in the *Ægyptian* Hieroglyphicks, the Alphabets of different Nations, fome Bas-Reliefs, Trophies, Rings, Cameos, Vafes, Urns, Ornaments of Architecture, and ancient Infcriptions and Epitaphs.

G 3   The

The 2d, fome Pieces relating to the an-cient *Hebrews*, with a Collection of Fefti-vals, Medals, and antique Statues.

The 3d may contain the two Books of the Marquis *Juftiniani*'s Gallery, which are full of antique Pieces ; and the *Trajan* Co-lumn, which is the moft entire Piece of Antiquity extant.

The 4th may fhew us the Decay of Painting and Sculpture, during 1100 Years that the Empire was on the Decline; from *Conftantine*, to the End of the fifteenth Century ; and fhould be compofed of a great Number of Pieces in the *Grecian*, *Ægyptian*, and *Gothick* Stiles, taken from the old Paintings, Tombs, Medals, Seals, and Tapeftry.

The 5th may be the Books, intitled, *Roma Subterranea*, filled with Pieces, in the Decline of the Empire, of the *Gothick* Stile.

The 6th fhould be the Sequel of the De-cay of the Arts, with feveral Pieces from wooden Plates, which fhew us the *Rudenefs* of their Defigns, fince the Invention of Printing.

The 7th may be the Original of the Art of *Engraving*, about the Year 1490 ; con-taining many Pieces of the firft and moft ancient Engravers ; as of *Ifrael*, and *Mar-tin Tedefco*, the Mafter of *Albert Durer* ;

of

of *Daniel* and *Jerom Hopfer*, and several others.

The 8th, the Works of *Albert Durer*, the Reftorer of Painting, and great Perfecter of Engraving in *Germany* and the *Low-Countries*, about the Year 1520.

The 9th, a Sequel for the Works of the *German* and *Low-Country* Mafters, containing fome Pieces of *Lucas* of *Leyden*.

The 10th may be filled with Pieces engraven on Wood, done in *Germany*, fince 1500, to this Time, as well by *Lucas Cranis*, *Jacob Pens*, *Holbeins*, *Hans Schauf-flig*, as others.

The 11th may be a Series for *Germany* and the *Low-Countries*, containing fome Pieces of thofe, which are called the *Leffer Mafters*; that is to fay, of *George Pentz*, *Aldegraef*, *Sebalde*, *John D'hifpanien*, his Brother, of *Virgilius Solis*, and others, whofe Names and Marks are unknown.

The 12th fhould be compofed of the Works of *Francis Floris*, who is called the *Flemifh Raphael*, and thofe of *Martin Hemfkirk*.

The 13th fhould be a Sequel for *Germany* and the *Low-Countries*, containing fome Pieces of *Lambert Suave*, *Lambert Lombard*, of *Peter Brughel*, *John Mabufe*, *M. Quintin*, *George Behan*, *Gilles Maffart*, and *Gilles Coignet*, of *Otho Venius*, *Cornelius*

Cort,

Cort, and *Theodore Bernard* of *Amfterdam*, of *Francis Klein*, a *Dane*, and of *John Strada*.

The 14th fhould be ftill a Sequel for *Germany* and the *Low-Countries*, containing fome Pieces of *Charles Mander*, and *Francis Pourbus*, of *Diterlin*, and *Lambert Lenoir*, *H. Utouch*, *Denis Calvaert*, *Abraham Janffens*, of *Paul Morelfer*, *Nicholas Hoey*, *Geldorp*, *Goltzius*, *Jofua* of *Monpre*, *John Hæfnaghel*; *Gerard* of *Groningben*, *Cornelius Vanfichem*, *John Bol*, *David Van Boons*, and *Peter Vander-Borcht*.

The 15th fhould contain fome of the Works of *Henry Hubart*, and *James Julius Goltzius*.

The 16th fhould be the Works of *William* and *Crifpin de Pas*, of *Magdalen* and *Barbara de Pas*, and of feveral others of that Name.

The 17th fhould be ftill a Suite for *Germany* and the *Low-Countries*, comprifing fome of the Works of *Nicholas de Bruyn*, of *Theodore de Bry*, and of *James de Ghein*.

The 18th fhould comprehend the Works of *John*, *Raphael*, *Juftus*, and *Gilles Sadalaer*, and alfo thofe of *Martin de Vos*.

The 19th fhould be ftill a Suite for *Germany* and the *Low-Countries*, and contain fome Pieces of *Anthony* and *Jerom Wierx*,

of

of *Lucas Vofterman, Valdor, John Saënre-dam,* of *John* and *Herman Muller, James Mathan, Simon Phrygius, Bartholomew Do-lende,* of *Mirevelt,* and the *Bolfwert*'s, of *Michael Snyders, Baptift Urintz, Hans Bol,* Peter and *Gerard de Sode,* of *Affuerus Lon-derfeel,* and of *Adrian Collaert.*

The 20th fhould be another Suite of Mafters that flourifhed in *Germany* and the *Low-Countries,* in the Beginning of the 17th Century ; *viz.* of *Jofeph Heintz, John* of *Vingth, John Abhach, John Rotten-bamer,* of *M. Kager,* Peter *Candide,* and *Dominick Cuftos,* of *Chriftopher Schuvarts, John Speccard,* and *Gerard Seghers,* of *Bar-tholomew Spranghers, Abraham Bloemaert, Anthony Van Dyck,* of *Abraham Brower, Gerard Honthorft, James Jordaens,* and of *Robert* Prince *Palatine.*

The 21ft fhould be the Works of Sir *Peter Paul Rubens,* a famous Painter of the *Low-Countries.*

I would fill the 22d with the Reprefen-tations of Night, and other dark, gloomy Pieces of various Mafters of all Nations ; as of *L. Gouth, J. Velde, Wittembrouck, Rembrant, Vanvliet,* and others.

The 23d fhould be a Collection of di-vers Landfkips, done by Mafters of diffe-rent Nations, that is to fay, of *Paul* and *Matthew Bril,* of the *Sadalaers,* Peter *Ste-*

phano,

phano, *Cornelius Corneli*, *Roeland Savery*, of *Monperche*, *Claude of Lorrain*, of *Fouquieres*, *Perelles*, of *Frederick Scalberge*, *Som*, and the *Nains*, and feveral others; to which may be added the Pieces of *Ruins*, of *Henry* of *Cleves*, *Michael Colyns*, and *Newland*; with fome Sea-Pieces, and maritime Profpects.

The 24th fhould be ftill another Suite of different. Landfkips, *viz.* by *Peter* and *John Brughel*, *Londerfeel*, *J. Velde*, *Tobit Verdach*, *Vandeboons*, *Merian*, and others.

The 25th, in order to fee the Re-eftablifhment of the Arts of Sculpture and Engraving, fhould contain fome Pieces of the firft Painters and Engravers, as of *Anthony Pollarolo*, *Andrew* and *Benedict Mantegna*, of *Dominick Campagnola*, *John* of *Brefcia*, and *James* of *Verona*; as alfo of feveral ancient Engravers, whofe Pieces are only known by their Marks; as the Mafters of the Name of *Jefus*, *Mercury*, the *Crab-Fifh*, the *Bird*, the *Star*, and feveral others; to which I would alfo add, fome Pieces of the firft *Italian* Painters; as of *Giotto*, *Ghirlandaio*, of *Hercules* of *Ferrara*, of *Peter* of *Perugia*, the Mafter of *Raphael*, and of *Giorgione*, the Mafter of *Titian*.

The 26th fhould be a Suite of the *Italian* Mafters, containing only fome of the Works

Works of *Raphael* of *Urbin*; and thofe engraven only by *Mark Antonio*, and *Auguftin* of *Venice*.

The 27th, a Suite of the Works of *Raphael*, engraved by the ancient Mafters, from 1530, to 1560 ; that is to fay, by *Julius Bonaffone, Sylvefter* and *Mark* of *Ravenna, Beaitrix* of *Lorrain*, and others.

The 28th fhould contain fome Pieces of *Michael Angelo*.

The 29th fhould be another Suite of the Works of the *Italian* Mafters, containing fome Pieces of *Anthony* of *Corregio, Francis Matzuolo*, firnamed *Parmigiano*, and *Polydore* of *Caravagio*.

The 30th, the Works of *Titian*.

The 31ft fhould contain the Works of *Julio Romano*, the *Caracci*, and *Perin del Vaga*, engraved by *John B.* of *Mantua*, and *Diana*, his Daughter ; as alfo by *Theodore-Ghifi*, and *George Julius* of *Mantua*.

The 32d fhould be compofed of the Works of the Painters and Sculptors, that were Contemporaries of *Raphael* and *Michael Angelo*, to the End of the 16th Century, *viz.* of *Baccio Bandinello*, the *Salviati*, of *Balthazar Peruzzi, Dominico Beccafumi*, of *Sodam* of *Sienna, Pordenone; Marcellus Venufto*, and *Baptift*, a Monk of the Order of *Camaldoli*.

The

The 33d fhould contain fome Pieces of *Thaddeus* and *Frederick Zucchero*, of *Daniel* of *Volaterra*, *Mark* of *Sienna*, and *Baptift Del Moro*.

The 34th, fome Pieces of *Paul* of *Verona*, *Paul Farinate*, the *Baffans*, of *Tintoret*, *Baptift Franco*, of *Mutiano*, and the elder and younger *Palma*.

The 35th, fome Pieces of thofe, who flourifhed between the Year 1550, and the End of the 16th Century, *viz.* of *Æneas Vico*, *Martin Rota*, and *Reverdino*, of *Camillo Proccacini*, *Baptift Fontana*, of *Cornelius Cort*, *Paffaro*, and *Sebaftian* of *Venice*.

The 36th, a Suite of the Works of the *Italian* Engravers, who flourifhed towards the latter End of the Sixteenth, and the Beginning of the Seventeenth Century; that is to fay, of *Cherubino Alberto*, *Villamena*, of *Raphael Schiaminofa*, and the *Tomafini*.

The 37th fhould contain the Pieces of *Francis Vanius*, *Ventura*, *Salembeni*, of *Civoli*, *Michael Angelo*, *Caravagio*, and the three *Caracci*.

The 38th fhould be a Suite of the Works of the *Italian* Painters of the feventeenth Century, *viz.* of the Capuchin Friars, *Piazzo*, and *Cofmo* of *Caftel Franco*, of *Hippolitus*, *Scarzelin*, of *Schiavone*, *Cangiage*, *Borgian*,

Borgian, Charles of *Venice, Pafqualin* of *Verona, Alexander Cafolani, Bernard Caftel-lo, Vefpafian Strada, Anaftafius Fontebuono, Francis* of *Viterbo, Luke Ciamberlani, Andrew* of *Ancona,* of *Anthony Pomerange,* of *Matthew* and *Frederick Greuter,* of *Philip* of *Naples,* and *Stephen della Bella.*

The 39th, a Suite alfo of the Works of the Painters and Sculptors, that flourifhed in *Italy,* during the feventeenth Century; that is to fay, of Cavalier *Jofepino, Guercino, Cirano, Francis* the *Fleming,* and *Marcel* of *Provence,* the Reftorer of *Mofaick* Painting, of *Gentilèque, Valentin, Edward Fialetti,* of *Peter Beretino* of *Cortona, Dominichino,* and *Guido Reni.*

The 40th fhould be to fhew the Re-eftablifhment of Painting in *France,* and contain fome Pieces of *René,* King of *Sicily,* of *Leonard da Vinci, Andrew del Sarto,* and *Roffo.*

The 41ft fhould be a Suite of fome of *Primaticcio's* Works, engraved by *Leo* of *Avefnes,* and *Anthony Jantus,* his Engravers; as alfo fome Pieces of *Jeffery* of *Moutiers, Leonard* of *Limoges, Stephen* of *Lofne, René Boivin, Luke Penis, Dominick* of *Florence,* and *Leonard Thury.*

The 42d may be filled with the Works of *John Coufin, John Genet,* of *Swifs,* of *Little Bernard, Peter* of *La Tour, Laurence* the

the *Glazier,* *Juſtus* of *Egmont,* and of ſeveral others, engraved in *France,* ſince the
Commencement of the ſixteenth Century.

The 43d ſhould contain ſome Pieces of
thoſe Maſters, who flouriſhed at the latter
End of the ſixteenth Century, and during
the Reign of *Henry* the IV. and *Mary* of
Medicis, *viz.* of *Freminet du Breuil, Bur-
net, Caron, du Bois, Lallemand, Thomas de
Leu, Leonard Gualtier,* and others.

The 44th, the Works of thoſe Maſters,
who flouriſhed about the Middle of the
ſeventeenth Century, that is to ſay, of
*James Blanchard, de Rabel, Ferdinand,
Iſaias Fournier, John Lis, Faber* and *Mal-
lerac,* of *Ruelle, Bellange,* and *James Callot.*

The 45th ſhould alſo be compoſed of
the Works of *James L'homme,* of *Little
Francis, Vanmol, Mellin, Queſnel, St. Igny,
Joſſelin, Rouſſellet,* and *Peter Brebiette.*

The 46th may be filled with the Works
of the beſt *French* Engravers, *viz.* of *Claudius Mellan, Gregory Huret, Peter Daret,
Gilles Rouſſellet, Michael Laſne,* and many
others.

The 47th, with the Works of the moſt
eminent *French* Painters, that is to ſay, of
*Simon Voüet, Nicholas Pouſſin, James Stella,
Champagne, Bourdon, de la Hire, Vignon,
Loir, Charles le Brun,* and *Peter Mignard,*
engraved by the beſt Maſters.

The

The 48th, I would fill with the fineſt Pieces of the moſt celebrated Engravers of the ſeventeenth Century.

The 49th, 50th, &c. may contain a Collection of Pieces of different Maſters of all Nations, who have either been omitted or forgotten in the preceding Volumes, or have flouriſhed ſince the End of the ſeventeenth Century; as well as of others now living, whoſe Names I ſhall not ſpecify, having an equal Veneration for them all.

The Subjects of *Morality* will alſo form ſeveral Volumes, *viz.*

The 1ſt may contain ſome Emblems of the Chriſtian Worſhip.

The 2d may be the Repreſentations of the Virtues and the Vices, with their Symbols.

The 3d may contain a Collection of different Emblems, Fables and Enigmas.

The 4th, a Collection of the Devices of Popes, Kings, Prelates, Princes, Noblemen, and others.

And laſtly, the 5th may be compoſed of a Collection of Hiſtorical Emblems, Devices and Enigmas, relating to Love and Death.

The *Mixed Subjects* will alſo compoſe ſome Volumes, *viz.*

The

The firſt may be a Collection of the re-markable Women, mentioned in the Old and New Teſtaments.

The 2d of Holy Virgins, Martyrs, Fe-male Saints, beatified Nuns, &c.

The 3d and 4th may alſo be Collections of Chriſtian Empreſſes, Queens, and illuſ-trious Women of different Nations.

The 5th may be the Repreſentations of *Roman* Ladies, taken from the antique Statues, Buſtos, Bas-Reliefs, &c.

The 6th may contain a Collection of the Goddeſſes of the ancient Pagans; with ſome illuſtrious *Ægyptian, Grecian, Aſiatick, Perſian,* and *Mahometan* Ladies.

The 7th may be filled with the Portraits of Women, both ancient and modern, who were either imperfect, mad, or Proſti-tutes.

The 8th may comprehend a Collection of all Sorts of Hunting, Fiſhing, and Fow-ling Pieces; to which may be added, a Collection of all the Animals that are treat-ed of in the aforeſaid Pieces.

And laſtly, the ninth may be filled with a Number of all Sorts of humorous and groteſque Pieces; to which may be added, a Collection of all Sorts of Maſque-rades.

R E P E R.

REPERTORIUM

Sculptile-Typicum:

O R, A

Complete Collection and Explanation

Of the SEVERAL.

Marks *and* Cyphers

O F

ENGRAVERS, &c.

1. **HANS** *Schauflig*, that is, *John Schauflig* of *Nordlingen* in *Germany*. We find this Mark in a Folio Book, in which the Paffion, Refurrection, and Af-
cenfion

cenfion of our Lord are engraved, with Notes by *Ulderic Pinder*, printed at *Norimberg* in 1507. He engraved in the Manner of *Albert Durer*.

2. Stoltzius, he engraved in the *Gothick* Tafte.

3. *Michael Coxis*, his Mark of certain *Arabian* Stories in 68 Plates, dated different Years, one is in 1576.

4. *Noel Garnire*, Engraver of Grotefques, Ornaments, and Figures, particulary of Arts in 48 Pieces.

5. *Domenico Campagnola*, a *Venetian*, and Scholar to *Titian*; we meet with fome of his Pieces engraved in 1518. His Brother *Julio* was alfo an Engraver.

6. *Michael*

6. **M** *Michael le Blon,* of *Frankfort,* died in *Amsterdam, Anno* 1650.

7. **B** *Renè Boivin,* engraved several Plates of antient Foliages.

8. **IBM** *John Maria da Brescia,* a Carmelite Friar, in 1502 he engraved a Virgin sitting in the Clouds, and underneath, three Saints of the Order of the Carmelites. He had a Brother called *John Anthony da Brescia,* who marked his Plates, with the Letters Jo. AN. BX. 1538.

9. **AF** *Micarino,* an Engraver in the *Gothick* Manner.

10. **M3** *Matthew Zagel,* engraved several Ornaments, and Grotesque Pieces, *per lo traverso,* or with Cross Strokes; he lived in 1500.

11. *Gaspar*

11. Ⓡℱ *or* ℂℬ   *Gafper Reverding*
or *Ravenfiein* ; his Pieces are lafcivious,.
and two of them reprefent Curtezans fport-
ing together.

12. D⧓V   *Dirich-Vander-Staren,*
lived in 1500.   He marked his Plates with
the Month and Year in which they were
engraved ; as in that of the Flood, and
another where the Virgin is aloft, and St.
Bernard at her Feet; marked 3d *Oct.*
1524, and the other marked *Anno* 1544.
He likewife ufed the Letter D in which was.
a V.

13. HE⌐ROM   *Hieronymus Mo-
cetus*, he publifhed the Refurrection of our
Saviour, and feveral Battles.

14. ⋈   *Anthony Vuormace*, a Painter
of *Cologn*, lived *Anno* 1529. He engraved
the Twelve Apoftles, in a ftanding Pofture.

15. *Vuaer*

15. I⋈H *Vuaer Van Hoffanen,* engraved 12 Round Plates of the Paffion, and underneath various Symbols of our Saviour. He likewife engraved the Life of Chrift in 60 Plates.

16. *Philip Adler Paticina* with this Mark marked on *S. Chriofaftnus.*

17. ₵$ *or* ₵$ *Cornelius Sichen,* ufed thefe two Marks in 108 Plates of the Old Teftament, 1569.

18. An unknown Mark on feveral Grotefque Pieces. This Mark differs very little from Number 55, which is alfo unknown.

19. V$ *or* N$ *Virgilio Sole* engraved a great many Pieces in Copper and Wood, in *Hifbin*'s Tafte. He engraved the Old and New Teftaments in 200 Plates ; the Metamorphofes of *Ovid* in 170 fmall Plates ;

Plates; Hunting-Pieces in great and ſmall,
&c.   He ſometimes made the Letter V on
one Side of the Plate, and S on the other.
See Number 61.

20. **ⅮⒷ**   *A. D. Bruin,* in 1560,
He engraved Six of the Twelve *Cæſars,*
and various Ovals in 1579.

21. **LH**   *Lambreckt Hopfer,* a *German,* engraved all kinds of Subjects: Some-
times his Mark is a Vaſe of Flowers in the
midſt of the Letters L.H, or the perpendicular Stroke of the L in the ſecond Stroke
of the H. He engraved 27 Pieces on the
Paſſion.

22. ⫿ⓒ⫿ⓒ⫿△⫿ⓒ⫿ *Adrian Collaert,*
he uſed various Marks, either in the Old
Teſtament, in Ornaments, in Freezes,
Stories, Groteſque Subjects, or Deaths
which are dragging away ſeveral Perſons.

23. Cormet

23. ℭℳℰ *Cormet* made this Mark in Small Subjects of two Figures each, both Lame, and a Charity with her three Children.

24. ℳℰ *Martin Hemſkirk*, his Mark in various Ornaments, in one of which are ſeveral Moles or Wants, 1548.

25. VY Theſe two Marks are in various Figures between Niches and Architecture of Chappels.

26. ℭℒ *Luke Van Cranogio*, or *Luke Van Craen*, Painter to the Duke of *Savoy*. His Mark is ſometimes L C, with a winged Dragon, and the Year 1509. At other times his Mark is two little *Gothick* Shields, or with the Mark in Number 35, or L. V. C. He engraved in Wood and Copper.

27. A

27. NⱢVM A Mark placed over feveral Ornaments of *Gothick* Architecture.

28. Aℬⅅ *or* Ⅾℬ *or* Nℬ

Nicholas de Bruyn, he ufed three Marks, in different Times.

29. ⅅⱽℰ *Cuerenhert*, his Mark in feveral *Turkifh* Stories, and various Subjects invented by *Martin Hemfkirk.*

30. ᴀⅅ *Albert Durer*, of *Norimberg*, Painter and Engraver, his Mark : He alfo ufed the Mark A. F. but in very few Plates. *John Burckmayr Auguftano* made ufe of the former Mark ; and *Matthew Grunevald*, of *Afchaffemburgh*, who - was Contemporary with *Durer* ; as alfo *Mark Antonio Raimondi*, in the Life of Chrift, copied from that of *Albert Durer*, for which the latter accufed him before the Senate of *Venice.*

31. *Hifbel*

31. **ISB** *Hisbel Peun,* an Engraver of *Norimberg,* called *Hisbin :* He ufed this Mark from 1513 to 1549. *Hans* (or *John*) *Sebald Beham* alfo ufed the fame Mark in his Plates. Some are of Opinion, that the Mark at Number 141 is *Hisbin's* Mark. Others, that there were two Engravers of the fame Name, and that their Marks differ'd by changing B in P. See in the *Abcedario Pittorico* for *Hans Sebald,* Page 220.

32. **TGT** *Albert Aldegraft,* of *Weft-phalia,* a famous Engraver.

33. **IGB** *Hans Brefanck,* engraved the Stories of the New Teftament ; and in 1619, the Twelve Apoftles, our Saviour, and St. *Paul.*

34. **Ƚ** *or* **Ƚ** *Lucas Van Leyden,* a celebrated Painter and Engraver, ufed thefe two Marks; in fome of his Plates we fee Part of the Mark at Number 133.

H 35. *Hans*

35. ISK   *Hans   Kaldung's*   Mark,
which alfo was ufed by *Luke Van Cranogio,*
but for what Reafon is not known.   See
Number 26.

36. HB   *Hans Baldung,* or *Balduin,*
in a Plate reprefenting Horfes, engraved in
1534.   The fame Mark was ufed by *Hans
Brofamer,* in his Plates of *Curtius* riding into the Gulph, in his *Laocoon,* and *Solomon*
worfhiping the Idol.   *Horatio Borgiano*
likewife made ufe of the fame Mark in
his Plates, and fometimes made an H and
a B.

37. MB   *Joft Ammon,* made much
fuch a Mark.

38. CAT   *Cornelius Heviffen.*

39. M α S *Martin de Secu*, of *Romerfiolaen*; he alfo marked his Plates thus, M + S.

40. P *Periecouter*, his Mark in feve- ral Figures in a ftanding Pofture, engraved in 1535.

41. DIF *Daniel Mignot fecit.*

42. M *Peter Mercand.*

43. R *or* Q *Peter Quaft*, has two Marks, making a P and Q. At other Times his Mark was *P. Quaft*, as in cer- tain Grotefque Pieces.

44. PG *George Pens*, Painter and En- graver of *Norimberg*, together with *Mark Antonio Raimondi*, engraved the Works of *Raphael* in *Rome*. He engraved after *Alde- graft's* Manner, his Mark was fometimes G. P. 1554.

H 2   45. The

45. The Mark on a Dead
Chrift, under which is written *Jean Ladefpeldrickt invenit*. The fame Mark is found
on other Pieces.

46. *Peter Cottart*, an Engraver
of Vafes.

47. *or* *Andrew An-
dreani* of *Mantua*, he made ufe of thefe
two Marks. He engraved on Wood, *a
tre tagli*, or three Croffings in his Shades.
The fecond Mark is found in the Triumph
of *Julius Cæfar* in 10 Sheets, engraved in
1599, and was invented by *Andrew Mantegna*, who alfo engraved on Copper. *Andrew Andreani* was called *il Piccolo Alberto*,
or *Little Albert*.

48. *Cornelius Bus*, or *Bofs*.

49. The

49. **HE** The Mark of certain Prints of Satyrs, and naked Figures under Trees.

50. **NW** A Mark under certain Pieces of Foliages and others, in the *Arabic* Tafte, 1535.

51. **DW** A Mark under a Chrift fupported by two Angels, 1555.

52. **A** A Mark under certain Anatomical Figures.

53. **B** *Peter Voeriot* of *Lorrain*, Engraver of Portraits.

54. **Mor K** *Bofs*, or *Bofche*, ufed thefe two Marks, different from *Cornelius Bofs*.

55. A

55. A Mark on the Twelve Apoſtles in a ſtanding Poſture, in large Sheets. This Mark differs but very little from Number 18.

56. F S   A *Gothick* Mark un-der *Lazarus* riſing from the Dead.

57. *Agoſtino Pariſino*, uſed this Mark.   He engraved the 81 Images de-ſigned by *Florio Macchi*, which are found in a Book, intitled, *The Emblems of* Paul Macchi.

58. *Hans Lutenſach*, who in 1560 engraved in a Book for the Nuptials of the Emperor *Ferdinand*, Tilts, Tourna-ments, and Rejoicings, in *Callot's* Manner.

59. A Mark under ſeveral Landſkips, in one of which is a Man on Horſeback killing a Dragon; 'tis alſo found under ſome little Pieces in which Chriſt's

Chriſt's Paſſion is engraved. See Number 154.

60. ⚹ *John Schorel's* Mark under the Twelve different Labours of *Hercules.*

61. ⚹ *Virgilio Sole*, of *Bruſſels*, under a dead Chriſt, engraved on a large Plate in 1542. See Number 19.

62. ⚹ The Mark found in an Old Teſtament in 50 Sheets, ſome of which are marked S. F. 'Tis likewiſe found in 105 Plates of the *Roman* Wars, and in 129 on different Subjects, with *Latin* Characters at Top and Bottom. This Artiſt likewiſe uſed the Mark I. A.

63. ⚹ A *Gothick* Mark.

64. ⚹ The Mark on a Print repreſenting a Satyr piercing a Prieſteſs of *Bacchus* with an Arrow.

H 4   65. *Theodore*

65. 乃ō *Theodore Zaghel*, his Mark in a Woman with her Back towards you.

66. 丹Œ A Mark in an *Adam* and *Eve*.

67. ℕŒ A Mark in a Peasant, who endeavours to break a Bough from a Tree.

68. P
VE A Mark under the Four Evangelists.

69. ℛ L *Renè*, or *Renato Lochon*, under several Portraits and Works of *Polidore*, 1651.

70. G L *Leonard Gaultier*.

71. *Peter*

71. **P** *Peter Lombardi*, he engraved the Works of Monſieur *Sampagna*.

72. **IC** *John Covay*, engraved the Works of Mr. *Vovet*, and others.

73. **FC** *Francis Chuveau*, engraved a great many Plates.

74. **PD** *Peter Daret*, engraved various Subjeĉts and Portraits.

75. **ML** *Michal l' Aſne*, engraved the Rudiments of Deſigning, and other Plates.

76. **FP** *Francis Perier*, Painter and En-graver, publiſhed ſeveral *Roman* Antiquities 1635, as in the Index of *Roſſi*'s Plates.

77. **HF** A Mark in certain *Gothick* Pieces dated 1545.

78.

78.   79.

80.   81.

82.

83. *J. F. Zabello*, a famous De-figner of *Bergamo*, 1546.

84.   85.

86.   87.

88. The Marks, or Characters, from Number 78 to 88, are found in certain *Gothick* Plates.

89. *Jacinto*

89. **Ġ** *Jacinto Giminiani,* of *Piſtoja,* Scholar to *Peter da Cortona.*

90. **M** The Mark of a certain Merchant, who bought a great Number of Copper Plates, under which he ſometimes put the Letters A. S. *excudit. Anthony Salamanca* likewiſe made uſe of the ſame Mark.

91. **ṢM** & **Æ** Theſe two Marks are in Twelve Pieces copied from the Paintings in the Chappel of *Fontainbleau*; on one Side is the firſt Mark, ſignifying *S. Martin* of *Bologna,* who was *Franceſco Primaticcio,* called Abbot of *S. Martin*'s; on the other is the ſecond Mark, which ſtands for *Anthony Guernier* the Engraver. The Reader will hereafter meet with the other Marks uſed by *Abbot Primaticcio.*

92. **Ṣ** *Adamo,* a Sculptor of *Mantua,* engraved the Angles of *Michael Angelo Buonaroti,* in ſeveral Plates, and worked for other Maſters.

H 6

93. Theſe

93. **GMF** *or* **MN** Thefe
two Marks were ufed by *Giorgio Ghifi*, of
Mantua ; he fometimes put *Ghifi-Mantovan
fecit.*

94. **F** *Stephen Colbenftagh Sc. Romæ* ;
he engraved the Paintings of *Domenichino*.

95. **G** *Gio. Benedetto Cafiglioni*, of
Genoa, a famous Painter and Engraver of
all Subjects.

96. **P** *or* **P** *Peter Tefta*, of
Lucca, a Painter and copious Engraver,
ufed thefe two Marks. He was Scholar to
Peter da Cortona.

97. **XX** The Mark of a Nativity, copied from *Parmigiano*, engraved by *Luke
Kilian.*

98. **MF** *or* **▭** *Andrew
Mantegna*, of *Mantua*, or *Padua*, Painter
and

and Engraver, his Marks: The second
Mark is found in the 10 Plates of the Triumph of *Julius Cæsar*, engraved by himself,
and afterwards cut in Wood in 1599, by
Andrew Andreani of *Mantua*, as we observed in Number 47.

99. Mor   *Mark Anto-*
nio Raimondi, of *Bologna*, called of *France*,
Raphael Urbin's Engraver, his Marks;
which Pieces he marked with the Letters
R. S. M. F. intimating by the two first
Letters, *Raphael Sancio*, by the two last
Marco Francia, or *Marco fecit*. He like-
wise employed other Marks, *i. e.* B. S.
signifying *Bononienfis* Sculptor. In his
Plates copied from *Buonaroti* he put MI.
AG. FLO. *i. e. Michael Angelus Florenti-*
nus; and afterwards for his own Mark he
employed that of *Mantegna*, expressed in
Number 98, which in like manner may
also signify *Marcus Antonius fecit*. In the
Life of Christ engraved by him, and co-
pied from the Plates of *Albert Durer*, of
Venice, he marked the Leaves with *Albert*
Durer's Mark.

100. Che-

100. **C̄B** or **C̄A** *Cheru-
bino Alberti Borghegiano*, that is, *da Borgo
S. Sepolcro*, ufed thefe two Marks. He engraved the Works of *Raphael*, *Michael
Angelo*, *Polidore*, and others.

101. ℛ *Silveftro da Ravenna*,
Mark Antonio's Scholar and Imitator, from
1535 to 1560. He employed himfelf
wholly in engraving the Pieces of *Raphael*
and *Julio Romano*.

102. **B** or **C̃in** The firft of
thefe Marks is of *Bernardo Caftelli*, a *Genoefe* Painter and Inventor. The fecond of
Camillo Congio, an Engraver, whofe Mark
was alfo C. C. *fecit*.

103. **V̊** *Lewis Valefio*, of *Bologna*, Painter and Engraver; his Mark was
alfo VAL.

104. *Raphael*

104. **R S A** *Raphael Scaminoſſi,*
Painter and Engraver.

105. **FF** *Odoardo Fialetti fecit.*
He was a Painter and Engraver of *Bologna.*

106. **ℛ or ℛ** Two different
Marks uſed by *Salvator Roſa,* a *Neapolitan*
Painter and Engraver.

107. **MF** A Mark under a St.
Sebaſtian engraved by *Michael* of *Lucca,*
after the Manner of *Michelagnoleſco,* 1550;
and we find the ſame Mark in a *Madona* of
Raphael, and after it, *ERRY. exc.*

108. **BP** *Bernard Paſſero,* an Engraver of all Subjects.

109. *Martin*

109. MR   *Martin Rota Sabinenſe,*
ſometimes marked with theſe Words, *Sa-*
benzanus fecit.

110. &   *Lucà Penni Romano,* or
Luca P. R. was *Raphael Urbin*'s Scholar,
and Brother to *Fattorino* ; he invented very
beautiful Subjects, which were engraved by
Giorgio Ghiſi of *Mantua* in 1556.

111. HG   *Henry Goltzius :* This celebrated *Dutch* Engraver imitated the Manner of ſeveral Maſters who lived before
him. He engraved *Raphael*'s Paintings,
and thoſe of other Maſters.

112. JG   *James Grand' Homme,* engraved the Portraits of the *Hereſiarchs,* and
others after *Rembrandt*'s Manner ; at other
times he marked thus, *J. G. Van Uliet.*

113. B   *Cornelius Berghem,* or *Ber-*
chen, is ſomething like the Mark 102.

114. The

114. The Mark of *Albert Fla-men* in certain Plates of Birds, Beaſts, and Fiſhes. *Alexander Badiali*, a Painter and Engraver of *Bologna* ; and *Anthony Boſs*, a Native of *France*, likewiſe uſed this Mark.

115. Two Marks of *Peter Vander Nelpe*, an Engraver of all Sub-jects.

116. *Theodore Van Tulden*, likewiſe an Engraver of all kinds of Sub-jects.

117. *Francis Villamena*, of *Aſ-ſiſi*, an excellent and expeditious Engraver. He likewiſe uſed the following Letters, F. V. F. or *F. Villam. F.*

118. *David Van Boons, Inv.* and after this Mark we read *Oons* ; his Plates were engraved by *P. Servator Sc.*

119. *1 G.*

119. *I G. Bronchorst*, in certain Landſkips, in which we likewiſe find the Letters C. P. *i. e. Cornelius Polemburgh pinxit.*

120. L A or L *Luke Voſterman*, Painter and Engraver of *Antwerp*, was adviſed by *Peter Paul Rubens* to apply himſelf to engraving; he engraved the Works of the ſaid *Rubens*, as alſo thoſe of *Raphael*, and *Vandyck.*

121. or The Marks of *Hans Saenredam*, a *Dutchman:* He died in 1607.

122. *James de Ghein excudit*, at *Charles Mander*'s 1608.

123. The Mark of *Adam Ælſheimer*, who worked with *Peter Breughel.*

124. The

124. The Mark in certain Landſkips of *Henry Cliven* or *de Clef. Martin de Clef* alſo made uſe of this Mark.

125. This Mark is of *Schelde a Bolſwaert*, and was uſed by him when he had not a mind to ſubſcribe his own Name.

126. *Rembrandt* ; at other times he uſed to put *Van Rhin inv.* He was a Painter and Engraver.

127. Near this Mark we read *Olyn.* and theſe are Landſkips engraved by *J. Van-Velde.*

128. A Mark in certain Landſkips and Solitudes, ſignifying *Anthony Van Vuaterl* Inventor ; 'tis ſometimes joined with the firſt of the three Marks that follow next, *i. e.* H. S. P. made in one.

129: *Joſeph*

129.　🙰 ℙ or 𝔸 or 𝔯

Joseph Ribera, called *Spagnoletto,* ufed
thefe three Marks at different Times.

130.　🅱 The Mark of a Virgin en-
graved by *Cornelius Bofs,* and underneath
Michael Ange : inv. that is *Buonaroti.* See
Numbers 48 and 54.

131.　△𝑅 The Mark of a Virgin
Sitting, after the Manner of *Durer,* and
underneath 1510.

132.　𝕊 This Mark is under a fmall
Virgin ftanding on a Half-Moon.

133.　VXH A Mark un-
der a S. *Veronica,* holding the Holy Hand-
kerchief. The former Part of this Mark is
feen in fome Plates of *Lucas Van Leyden.*

134.　MⱧO *Mauro Oddi,* of
Parma, Engraver and Painter.

135. *Agoftino,*

135. ⟨mark⟩ *Agoſtino,* a *Venetian,* Scholar to *Mark Antonio Raimondi,* engraved at *Rome,* the Paintings of *Raphael, Julio Romano,* and others. He alſo marked with the Letters A. V. I. or A. V. 1525.

136. ⟨mark⟩ *or* ⟨mark⟩ *Stephen Della Bella,* of *Florence,* a famous and whimſical Engraver. His other Mark is S. B.

137. ⟨mark⟩ *Julio Ceſare Venenti,* an Engraver of *Bologna.*

138. ⟨mark⟩ *Joſeph Maria Metelli,* of *Bologna,* a famous and fantaſtical Engraver of all kinds of Subjects.

139. ⟨mark⟩ *Andrea Salmincio,* of *Bologna,* an Engraver, and *Valeſio's* Scholar.

140. *Do-*

140. **B** *Domenico Beccafumi Siennese,* a Painter and Engraver: We alſo find this Mark in certain Wooden Cuts, copied from *Titian*'s Paintings. He died in 1549.

141. **ISP** See Number 31, where we find pretty near the ſame Mark.

142. **CF** *Francis de Poilly,* engraved for ſeveral Maſters.

143. **AS** *Anthony Salamanca,* or *Ant. Sal. exc.* 1543.

144. **CF** The Mark of *Herman Coblent* under the Four Evangeliſts and other Plates ; one of *David,* of *Judith,* and *Lucretia* ; and afterwards *Adrianus Hubertus exc.* 1576.

145. **RU** *Raphael Urbin,* a celebrated Painter and Inventor, whoſe Piece wer were engraved by the greateſt Maſters. In the preſent Mark he gives the Initials of his Name and Sirname. See Number 99.

146. **ICI** *Hans Liefrinck,* who thus marked certain Plates repreſenting Birds and Hunting-Pieces, with Ornaments.

147. **BD** *Domenico Barriera,* of *Florence,* who going commonly by the Name of *Domenico Fiorentino,* marked ſome Plates D. F. 1647. The ſame Mark was uſed by *Domenico Bonavera,* an Engraver of *Bologna,* and *Domenico Bettini* a Painter, in his Pieces of Flowers and Animals.

148. **AE** *Anthony Tempeſta,* of *Florence,* a famous Engraver : His Mark was ſometimes a T. with an E. joined to the Leg of the T.

149. **IN** *Nicolas Beatrici Lotharingius fecit.*

150. *Theo-*

150. *Theodore Cruger,* or *Greuger,* Engraver.

151. *Andreas Vande-Venne pin-xit.* V V. *Delft. Sc.* that is, *Willielmus Delft Sculpfit.*

152. *Henry Van Cliven,* or *Cli-venfe,* or *de Clef,* a Painter of *Antwerp,* who died in 1589. See Number 124.

153. *Matthew Grunewald,* fir-named of *Afchaffemburg,* Painter and En-graver after the Manner of *Albert Durer;* he died in 1510.

154. The Mark of feveral little Plates, reprefenting our Saviour's Myfteries, engraved either by *Agnes Freij, Albert Durer's* Wife, or fome Scholar of his.

155. *Gio.*

155. Ⓒ Ⓑ Ⓘ *Gio.* or (*John*) *Batista Gal-*
leftrucci, of *Florence*, Engraver, inferted in
the Catalogue of *Roman* Painters, in the
Year 1652. He engraved feveral of the
Baffo-Relievos of *Polydore.*

156. Ⓡ Ⓖ Ⓕ *Guido Ruggeri fecit.*
The Mark of feveral Pieces painted at *Fon-*
tainebleau by Abbot *Primaticcio,* and engraved by the above-mentioned, who accompanied him into *France.*

157. Ⓢ Ⓥ The Mark of *Juftus Sa-*
dalaer. He fometimes ufed only this Mark;
at other times he added, *Sadalaer.* I. S.
exc. is the fame.

158. Ⓐ Ⓛ *Alexander Algardi,* Sculptor of *Bologna,* in a Conclufion engraved by
Francis de Poilly, 1653. He at other
times made ufe of the fame Mark, but
without the G.

I

159. *MF*   *Francis Maria Francia*, an Engraver of *Bologna*.

160. *ÆV*   *Æneas Vighi*, o1
Vico, of *Parma*. His other Marks are Æ
E. V. Æ. V.

161. *C×*   COUNT DE CAYLUS, o
Paris, his Mark, on his Engravings i1
Wood, &c. from the Drawings of th
greateft Mafters.

162. The Mark of *Crifpin Paj
fæus*, or *Crifpin de Pas*.

163. The Mark of *Charles A
bertus*, in a Book of Vafes from *Polydore*.

164. *Cafpar Luyken*.

165. Georg

165. G̲K̲   *George Keller.*

166. D̲T̲   *David Teniers.*

167. *Ƒ.Ƒ.*   *J.* Epiſcopus, **or** *Biſhop*
fecit.

168. C̲F̲   *Francis Cauveau.* See Number 73.

169. Hh   *Henry Hondius.*

170. ſMB   *St. Martin di Bologna.*

171. .S.
R̲A̲F̲   The Mark of *Raphael*
Schiaminoſſi de Burgo, on the Heads of our
Saviour, the Virgin *Mary,* and the Twelve
Apoſtles,

Apoftles, in 1606 and 1607, as big as the Life. See Number 104.

172. **DZ** Z. *Dolendo.*

173. **AE** *Anthony Tempefta's* Marks in a Book intitled, *in Quatuor Evangeliftas Arabicé & Latiné,* printed at *Rome.* See Number 148.

174. **A** *A. Genoels,* on his Landfkips.

175. **Weeuw** *Fecit,* upon feveral Prints from *Rubens.*

176. **WP** *Wenceflaus Hollar* Pragenfis excudit.

177. **DC** On the Plates in a Book in 12mo. intitled, *Liberatione di Vienna dall' Armi Ottomane, di Lotto Lotti. Parma* 1685.

178. On

178. $\mathcal{SC}$ On an Etching of our Saviour fainting under the Crofs.

179. $\mathbb{P}_F$ FE. *Hen: Cock* exc. 1570.

180. $\mathbb{P}$ 1536.

181. $A\!\!-\!\!B$ On the Senfes very fmall, 1569. See Number 20.

182. RB On two Prints, the Wife Men offering, and a Circumcifion, after the Manner of *Lucas Van Leyden.*

183. $\maltese\,RAB$ On the Plates of a Book in Quarto, intitled, *Medailles Antiques de Mr. Ant. de Pois.* Quarto.

I 3   184. *Claudio*

184. *Claudio Metelli*, on the 80 Plates of the Cries of *Bologna*, by *Hannibal Carracci*.

185. See Numbers 19 and 61.

186. *Ifrael Martin*, one of the firſt Engravers. *Albert Durer*, *Lucas Van Leyden*, and *Aldegraft*, were his Diſciples.

187. *Nicolas Andrea.*

188. *Alexander Badiale*, a Painter; the firſt of theſe Marks was uſed by *Anthony Boſs*. P.

189. *Jacobus Bink*, Painter and Sculptor.

190. *Pete*

190. *Peter Brebiette*, Painter.

191. C or CC inv. *Carlo*
Cignani, Painter.

192. *Stephanus Colbenstagh*,
much like Number 125.

193. DI. or R E *D. de Larmessin.*

194. HH *Hermannus Henr. Quiter.*

195. *Cornelius Vischer.*

I 4   196. *Thomaus*

196. ℭ *Thomaus Cookſon*, an *Engliſh* Engraver, uſed this Mark. Some of his Works bear date from 1609 to 1624.

197. *Rpf.* Two Marks made uſe of by PRINCE RUPERT, the firſt to a *Saracen's* Head, the latter to a Man with a Spear, both in Mezzotinto; to him we are indebted for that delicate Art.

198. *ÆEf* *John-Evelyn*, Eſq his Mark to five ſmall Prints of his Journey from *Rome* to *Naples*.

199. *John Vanſomer's*, which i ſometimes miſtaken for *Paul Vanſomer*.

200. 15 K 69 The Mark on *Michael Angelo's* laſt Judgment, of one Foo five Inches by one Foot ten Inches, *Romæ*

201. Th

201. B The Mark of *Bartholomew Breenbergh*, on Landſkips.

202. A⁄E A Mark on a Head of *Albert Durer*.

N. B. Number 62 is alſo the Mark of *Simon Frizius*; and Number 128 is alſo that of *Antonius Waterlo*.

The Initial Letters *used* *by* Engravers *for their* *Marks.*

AB. *These two Letters joined together, with an F issuing out from the B, is the Mark of* Alexander Badiale *of* Bologna, *Painter and Engraver.*

Ab. Bl. ⎫ inv. Abraham Bloemaert, *an inde-*
A. Bl. ⎭ *fatigable* Dutch *Engraver.*

A. Both. Andrew Both.

A. C. P.
A. C.
Agos. C.
Ag. C.
Ag. Bononiæ, ⎬ *Are all Marks of* Augustino Carracci *of* Bologna, *a celebrated Painter and Engraver.*

A. D. J. F. Anthony de Jacquart Fecit. *He engraved several Pieces.*

A. D. Bruin, *see Number* 20.

A. G. Albert Glockentonius, *in the Twelve Plates representing our Saviour's Passion.*

A. F. *A Mark found in some Plates of* Albert Durer, *see Number* 30.

I 6 A. L. P. I.

A. L. P. I. Anthony Licinio Pordenone inv. Edward Fialetti fc.

A. P. M. A. Abbas Primaticcius inv. Mark Anthony exc. *This Mark is found in a Plate reprefenting a Shepherd lying under a Tree ; and another holding his Hand on a univerfal Planifphere.*

A. S. *See Number* 90.

Æ. V. *See* E. V. *fignifying* Eneas Vighi, or Vico; *and fee Number* 160.

A. V.   } Agoſtino *the* Venetian.   *See*
A. V. I. }   *Number* 135.

B. John Sebald Beham. *See Number* 3 **.** *Abbot* Primaticcio, *who in* France *was called of* Bologna, *ufed the Letter* B *for his Mark.* 'T*was alfo ufed by* il Bonafoni, *and likewife by* Domenico Beccafumi, *interfecting it with a Line,   as in Number* 140.

BAL. SEN. Baldaffar Senefo, *i. e.* Baldaffar Peruzzi *of* Sienna.

B. B. Bartholomew Boham *of* Norimberg; *he engraved in* Rome, *and in* Bologna, *with* Mark Antonio Raimondi.   Bartholomew Bifcaino, *a* Genoefe *Painter, alfo ufed thefe Letters in fuch Plates as were of his own Invention.*

B. B. A. F. Baccio Bandinelli, *a* Florentine *Architect.*

Belli fecit.   James Belli. *See* J. B. F.

B. C

B. C. Equ. Bartholomew Coriolanus, *of* Bononia, *Knight*.

B. F. V. F. Baptiſt Francus Venetus fecit.

B. M. VVV. Bernardo Malpucci, *of* Mantua, *Painter and Engraver*; *he engraved in Wood with three Tools*; *with the firſt he made the* Profil, *with the ſecond the* Shadows, *and with the third the* Lights.

Bol. Inventor. ⎱Julio Bonaſoni, *of* Bo-
Bonaſo ſc. 1545. ⎰ logna.   *See* J. B. F.

B. P. Bartholomew Paſſarotti, *of* Bologna, *a Painter*.

B. S. Bartholomew Shenius, *or* Bononienſis Sculptor.

B. Z. 1581. Bern. Zan.

C. B. Cornelius Boſs. *This Artiſt engraved* Julio Romano's *Bacchanal.   See Number* 130.

C. Bl.   ⎱Cornelius Bloemaert, *Son of* A-
Corn. Blo. ⎰ braham *the famous* Dutchman.

C. Bleker. *The Mark of* Cornelius Bleker *in certain Hiſtorical Landſkips*, 1636.

C. C. Fecit. Camillus Congius. *See Number* 102. Charles Cignani, *of* Bologna, *Painter, Inv.   He alſo uſed two* C's, *the one within the other*.

C. D. F. Charles David Fecit.

Cl. Mell. ſc. Romæ.   Claudius Mellanus.   *See* M. inv.

C. L. fec. Caſpar Luyken fecit.

                                   C. P.

C. P. Cornelius Polemburgh pinxit.   John
Bronchorft inc. *See Number* 119. '

C. Schoenius, Martin Schoenio, *of* Calem-
bach, *Painter and Engraver, in the
Time of* Albert Durer. *He died in*
1486. *Some of the Curious think him to
be the same with* Buonmartino. *See Number* 39.

D. Domenichino, *of* Bologna, *a famous
Painter and Inventor.*

D. B. Bernard Gallo, *called the Short, en-
graved several Works, and among the reft*
Ovid's *Metamorphofes, and the Old and
New Teftament printed at* Lyons 1559.

D. F. Domenico *of* Florence. *See Number* 147.

D. H. David Hopfer, *Brother of* Lambert,
noted down in Number 21, *and of* Jerome ; *all three* German *Engravers.*

D. M. C. Domenico Maria Canuti, *a copious Painter of* Bologna. '

DO. CAP. 1518. Domenico Campagnola,
of Venice.

E. V. Eneas Vighi, *or* Vico, *of* Parma, *engraved the Works of* Roffi, Titian, Buonaroti,
Julio Clovio, *and of* Baccio Bandinelli.

E. V. H. Efaiah Van Hulfen.

F. B.

F. B. Francis Briccio, *of* Bologna, *Pain-ter ; he engraved the Pieces of* Lewis Car-racci.

F. B. B. Father Bonaventura Biſi, *of* Bo-logna, *called* il Padre Pittorino, *or the* Painting Fryar.

F. B. V. I. Frederic Barocci, *of* Urbino, inv. *He ſometimes, inſtead of the* I, *put* F, *that is,* Fecit.

Fr. Bol. Inv. Francis *of* Bologna Inventor, *that is, Abbot* Primaticcio.

F. C. Franceſchino Carracci, *of* Bologna, *younger Brother to* Auguſtin *and* Han-nibal.

F. L. D. Ciatres exc. *The Mark of a Dealer in Prints.*

F. P. Francis Primaticcio, *or* Franceſco Parmegiano, *who ſometimes put an* F *only, in his Wooden Cuts engraved with three Tools.*

F. P. J. V. Bonaſius. *Theſe Letters are found in a* Madonna *of* Franceſco Pri-maticcio, *engraved by* Julio Bonaſoni.

F. T. F. Flaminio Torre fecit. *He was a Painter and Engraver.*

F. V. B.

F. V. F.
F. Villam. F. } Francis Vanni Fecit. Fran-cis Villamena *uſed this and the following Mark. See Number* 117.

G. A.

G. A. *The Heirs of* John Agucchia.

G. F. Giorgio *of* Mantua Fecit. *In a Piece of* Primaticcio's *representing* Vulcan's *Forge. See Number* 93.

G. M. F. Giorgio *of* Mantua, *in other Pieces of the abovementioned* Primaticcio.

G. P. George Pens. *See Number* 44.

G. R. } Guido Reni, *of* Bologna, *a ce-*
G. R. F. } *lebrated Painter,* Fecit.

G. R. B. C. F. Guido Reni, *in the Overthrow of the Giants, engraved by* Bartholomew Coriolano.

G. S. F. Gio. *or* (John) Sirani Fecit.

Guil. Baur 1640, William Baur, *Painter to the Emperor.*

G. V. S. G. Van Scheindel Fec. *and* V. V. Buytuvech. inv.

Har. Holbenius. Holbenius *of* Haerlem.

H. B. *This Mark was used by* Hans Burckmair, *who engraved* 36 *Historical Pieces relating to the Empire* ; Hans Brosamer, *who lived in* 1538 ; *and* Horatio Borgiani *of* Rome. *See Number* 36.

H. Bol. Hans Bol, *i. e.* John Bol, *in certain Landskips.*

H. C. Hans Liefrink, *in certain Plates of Birds, and Parties of Hunting, in Freezes. See Number* 146.

H. H. Hans Holbein.

HO.

HO. FF. 1599. *In a Print of* Pharaoh's *Army drowned, by* Paul Farinati, *of* Verona.

H. S. 1558.   Hercules Septimius Mutinenfis.   *In certain Figures and Ornaments of Buildings.*

H. V. C. 1517.   Hans Van Culmhac, *was* Albert Durer's *Scholar.*

I. A.   *See Number* 62.

J. B.   James Binckius.   J. B. *and a Bird, is another Mark of a different Author in a* David, *who fets his Foot on* Goliah's *Head, after* Albert Durer's *Manner.*

J. Bonafo F. 1544.
J. B. F.
Julio. B.

}   Julio Bonafoni fecit.   *See other Marks at the Letter* B. *Bonafo* 1544, *was another of his Marks.*

J. B. M.   John Baptifta, *of* Mantua, *was Scholar to* Julio Romano ; *he engraved the Burning of* Troy, *and other Pieces of his own Invention.*

J. B. F.   James Belli, *a Frenchman,* fecit, *or* Belli fecit.

J. C. Proc. Inv.   Julius Cæfar Procaccinus Inventor.

J. G. Bronchorft.   *See Number* 119.

J. G. Van Uliet, *is the fame as* James Grand-homme.   *See Number* 112.

J. H.   Jerom Hopfer.

I. H.

I. H. W. 1570.

J. K. James Kerver.

I. L. 1712. J. Luyken.

I. M: Ifrael Meck, *in certain Subjects of the Paſſion, and other Plates.* See I. V. M. *The ſame Mark was alſo uſed by* Ifrae. Martino, *ſuppoſed to be the ſame with* Buonmartino, *who lived in* 1490.

L. fec. Joannes Livius fecit. *He engraved after* Rembrandt's *Manner.*

Jo. Guill. Baur. John William Baur. *See* William Baur.

Jo. AN. BX. John Antonius Brixianus 1538. *See Number* 8.

I. R. W.

J. S. Juſtus Sadalaer exc. John Saenredam *uſed the like Mark, joining the* J *to the* S *See Number* 121. *and* 157.

J. S. B. John Sebald Beham. *See* B, *and Number* 31.

I. V. M. Ifrael Van Mechelen, *or* Mechelini, *or* Van Meck, *and of* Lomazzo *ſurnamed of* Mentz ; *he lived before* Alber Durer, *and ſometimes marked his Plate with his Name* Ifrael, *only.*

L. C. Civ. F. *with the firſt* C *in the perpendicular Stroke of the* L, *is the Mark o* Ludovico Cardi, *ſurnamed* Civoli, *a* Florentine *Painter, in a Plate of the Suppe of the* Phariſee.

L. C

L. C. F. B.
Lod. C. I. Fr. Bri. } Lewis Carracci Inventor. Franceſco Briccio intaglio, *or engraved.*

L. C.
L. O. C. } Lewis Carracci, *in his three Plates engraved with his own Hand.*

L. D. *In a Sacrifice, and* Alexander *the Great, by Abbot* Primaticcio.

L. C.
L. V. C. } Luke Van Cranogio, *or* Luke Van Craen, *Painter of* Savoy, *Anno* 1509. *See Number* 26.

L. H. Lambert Hopfer. *See Number* 21.

L. K. A. Luke Kilian, *of* Augsburg, *engraved* Tintoret's *and* Spranger's *Works.*

L.
L. L.
L. S. } Lambert Lombard, *or* Suſterman, *or* Suavius, *all which ſignify the ſame Perſon.*

L. L.
Lollius. } Lorenzo Lolli, Guido Reni's *Scholar.*

Lucas P. R. Luke Penni, *the* Roman, Raphael's *Scholar. See* Number 110.

L. V. V. Luke Van Uden, *in ſome of* Titian's *Landſkips.*

L. Lucas *of* Leyden. *See Number* 34.

M. A. F. *See Number* 99.

M. C. Martin de Clef, *or* Clivenſis Auguſtanus.

M. D. Vos. Martin de Vos, *a celebrated Inventor for Engravers.*

Mel.

Mel. Gir. fec. Melchior Girardini fecit. *H*
was a Painter and Engraver at Rome.

M. G. Matthew Greuter, *Engraver, bor*
at Strafburg, *Ann.* 1566.

M. inv. ⎫ *Are all differen*
Mel. p. & fc. ⎬ *Marks of* Clau,
Mellan. ⎬ dius Mellan *of*
Mel. fc. Romæ. 1633. ⎭ *Paris.*

MI. AG. FLO. Michael Angelo, *of* Flo·
rence, *i. e.* Buonaroti.

M. L. Melchion Lorichius.

M. Merian. Matthew Merian.

M+S. Martin de Secu, *or* Schonio, *callec*
by fome Buonmartino, *was* Albert Durer'.
Mafter. See Number 39.

M. R. Mark - Ravennate, *or* Ravignano
i. e. Mark *of* Ravenna, *Scholar to* Marl
Antonio Raimondi. *See* R. S.

M. Z. Martin Zinkius, *i. e.* Zazingeri.
1500. *See Number* 10.

Nadat, *has marked his Plates with a* Moli
or Want-trap.

N. B. Nicholas de Bruyn. *See Number* 28

N. B. L. F. Nicholas Beatrici Lotharingiu:
fecit. *See Number* 149.

N. C. F. Nicholas Chapron, *a Frenchman*
fec. *Anno* 1649. *He engraved* Raphael'
Galleries, painted in the Vatican.

N. M. D. Nicholas Manuel de Berna, 1518

N P. *or* P N. Peter Nolin.

P. B. F

. B. F. } Paul Blancus fecit & incidit.
. B.

. C. Paul Caliari, *i. e.* Paul Veronefe, *Painter and Inventor.*

. F. Paul Farinati *of* Verona, *Painter and Inventor.*

. H. Peter Hys, *in certain Pieces of Devotion.*

'hil. Th. 1589. Philip Thomafini.

'. John Sebald Beham. *See Letter* B. *and the Letters* V. P.

'. Quaft. Peter Quaft. *See Number* 43.

'i. Ss. Bart. Peter Santi Bartoli, *Engraver, of* Perugino *in* Rome.

'. S. F. Peter Stefanoni fecit. *This Artift engraved the* Carracci's *Works.*

'. V. Borcht inv. & fc. Peter Van del Borcht.

ι. *The Mark of* Ravignano, *and underneath* R. V. I. *that is,* Raphael Urbino Inv. *See* MR.

ι. B. T. A. Robetta.

ι. S. M. A. } *See Number* 99.
ι. S. M. F.

ι. S. Ravignanus Sculpfit. *See* M. R.

ι. S. M. R. Mark *of* Ravenna. *He put this Mark to* Raphael Sancio Urbino's *Pieces.*

R. V. A. Gaudenfis Sculp. *The Mark of feveral Pieces invented by* Peter da Cortona.

S.

S.

S. B. Stephen della Bella *of* Florence.   S
Number 136.

S. B. D. Pictor. *Under an Annunciatio
invented by* Peter Candido.

S. C. Simon Cantarino, *called of* Pefar
Painter and Engraver.

S. C. F. Stephen Carteron fecit, 1616.

Sebenzanus fecit. *This is* Martin Rota
Sabina. *See Number* 109.

S. F. Simon Frifius fc. *Thefe are Portra
engraved by* Henry Hondius. *See Nu;
ber* 62.

S. G. S. Simon Guillain fc. *This Artift, v.
was born in* Paris, *engraved* 80 *differ;
Figures of* Hannibal Carracci, *called
Cries of* Bologna, *Anno* 1646.

S. P. Simon Paffeus.

S. P. F. Stephen du Perac fecit.

Strada.   Vefpafian Strada *of* Rome.

T. Anthony Tempefta *of* Florence, *Pai;
and Engraver. See Number* 148.

T. C. Theodore Cruger. *See Number* 1

VAL. Valefio, John Lewis Valefio
Bologna. *See Number* 103.

Van Rhin in. Rembrandt de Rein.
.   Number 126.

.V. C. Vincenzio Caccianemici, *a Noble;
of* Bologna, *and Painter.*

Vef. S. Vefpafiano Strada *of* Rome.

V. P. *or* B. *or* P. *or* J. S. P. *were four Marks ufed by* John Sebald Beham, *when he did not care to put his own Name, which is found Number* 31.

V. S. 1622. Valentine Sezenius. *The fame Mark was alfo ufed by* Virgilio Sole, *mentioned Number* 19.

V. S. I. Ventura Salimbeni, *of* Sienna, *Painter and Inventor.*

V. V. Delft. *See Number* 151.

V. C. V. *A Mark ufed by an antient Engraver in a St.* Bartholomew *and a St.* George.

W. D. H. Will. Henius.

W. H. Wenceflaus Hollar.

W. P. Will. Paffe.

Z. A. Zazingeri, *or* M. Z. Martin Zinkius, *as was before-mentioned.*

AN

A

Chronological and Historical Series of the most Eminent PAINTERS.

Masters, and their Countries.	Born, Died.	Whose Disciples, and in what they excelled.	Places of Residence, and principal Works.
Andrea Taffi, a *Florentine*, the Restorer of Mosaic in *Italy*.	1213 1294	*Apollonius*, a *Greek*. History and Mosaic.	*Florence*, where he did a Picture of Christ, 7 Cubits long.
Giunta Pisano, a *Grecian*, sent for to *Florence* by the Senate.	*Flo.* 1236	Some *Greek* Painter. History and Figures.	*Florence*, where in the great Church of the *Francifcans*, he painted the Death of that Saint, with this Inscription, *Juncta Pisanus fecit de mense Octobri, Anno* 1236. *India. 9.*

Cimabue, of a noble Family in Florence, the Father of Modern Painting.	1240 1300	Giunta Pisano and Arnolfo Tedesco. History and Architecture.	Florence, where he painted several Altar-pieces, and also built the Church of St. Mary Delsore.
Buonamico Buffalmaco, of Florence.	1262 1340	Andrea Taffi. History.	Arezzo and Pisa, where he painted the Abbey of St. Paul.
Margaritone, of Arezzo, Inventor of the Art of Gilding with Leaf-Gold on Bole-Armoniac.	Flo. 1275	History and Sculpture.	Rome and Arezzo, at the last of which he made the fine Tomb of Pope Gregory X.
Giotto, of a little Village near Florence, much improved the Art of Painting.	1276 1336	Cimabue. History, Architecture, Sculpture and Mosaic.	Rome and Florence; at the former he did the Mosaic Ship over the Portico of St. Peter's Church, and at the latter the Death of the Virgin, so much commended by Mich. Angelo.
Simone Memmi, of Siena, improved Giotto's Manner, by drawing after the Life.	1285 1345	Giotto. History and Portraits.	Rome and Florence, celebrated by Petrarch for the Portrait of his beloved Laura.

K

Masters, and their Countries.	Born, Died.	Whose Disciples, and in what they excelled.	Places of Refidence, and principal Works.
Taddeo Gaddi, of Florence, improved the Colouring and Livelinefs in Painting.	1300 1350	His Father Gaddo Gaddi, and Giotto. Hiftory and Architecture.	Florence and Arezzo; at the firft he built the famous Bridge, at the other painted the Paffion, in the Church of the Holy Ghoft.
Steffano Florentino, of the fame Place.	1302 1337	Giotto. Figures and Heads.	Florence and Rome; Naked Figures, of which he was the firft modern Painter.
Pietro Cavallino, of Rome, was efteemed a Saint for his great Piety.	1304 1379	Giotto. Hiftory, Mofaic, and Sculpture.	Rome; where in St. Paul's is the famous Crucifix of his making, which talked to St. Bridget.
Gaffaro Spinello, a Florentine.	Flo. 1330	Giotto. Hiftory.	Florence and Arezzo; at the laft is his Piece of the Fall of the Angels.
Ambrog: Lorenzetti, of Siena.	1330	Giotto. Hiftory and Landfkips.	Rome; he was the firft that painted Rains, Storms, and Winds.

Angelo Gaddi, of *Florence*.	1323 1387	Giotto, and his Father *Taddeo Gaddi*. History.	*Florence*.
Giacomo *Caffentino*, Founder of the Academy at *Florence*.	*Flo.* 1350	*Taddeo Gaddi*. History.	*Florence*, painted in the Chapel of the Academy the Picture of St. *Luke* drawing the Virgin, and on one Side all the Academists, which were Ten, and on the other their Wives.
Tomaso Giottino, of *Florence*.	1324 1356	Giotto, and his Father *Steffano Florentino*. History.	*Florence*.
Andrea Orgagna, of *Florence*.	1329 1389	History and Architecture.	*Florence* and *Pisa*.
Aleffio Baldovinetti, a *Florentine*.	1366 1448	History and Mosaic.	*Rome* and *Florence*.
Hubert *van Eyck*, of *Maseyck* on the *Meuse*.	1366 1426	History.	*Gaunt*, where is a Piece, the Subject taken from the *Revelations*, univerfally admired.
John *van Eyck*, of the same Place.	1370 1441	His Brother *Hubert*. History.	*Bruges*, where in 1410 he found out the Art of painting in Oil.

K 2

Masters, and their Countries.	Born, Died.	Whose Disciples, and in what they excelled.	Places of Residence, and principal Works.
Frate Filippo Lippi del Carmine, of Florence.	1371 1438	History and Portraits.	Rome, Naples, and Florence.
Pietro della Francesca, del Borgo S. Sepolcro, a Florentine.	1372 1458	History and Battles.	Rome and Florence.
Donatello, of Florence.	1383 1466	Architecture and Sculpture.	Florence.
Frate Giovanni Angelico da Fiesole.	1387 1455	Religious Subjects, large, and in Miniature.	Rome and Florence.
Filippo del Brunelleschi.	1387 1446	Architecture and Sculpture.	Florence, where he built the Cupello of St. Mary del Fiore's.
Francisco Antonello di Messina, the first who brought Painting in Oil into Italy.	1390 1480	John van Eyck. History.	Venice and Bruges.
Francesco Squarcione, of Padua, called the Father of Painting, because he had ...	1394 1474	History.	Padua.

Name	Date	Subject	Place
Masolino da Panicale.	Flo.		Florence.
Paolo Uccello, of Florence.	1432 Ob.	Perspective and Birds.	Florence.
Bartolomeo Bramantino, of Milan.	1432 Nat.	History and Architecture.	Milan and Rome.
Gentil da Fabriano, of Verona.	1400 Flo.	Giovanni da Fiesole. History.	Rome and Verona.
Giaccmo Bellini, of Venice.	1420 Nat.	Gentil da Fabriano. History and Portraits.	Venice.
Bartolomeo della Gatta Camaldolese, Abbate di S. Clemente Aretino.	1400 1481	History and Miniature.	Rome.
Benozzo Gozzoli, of Florence.	1400 1478 Flo.	Giovanni da Fiesole. History.	Florence.
Dominico Venetiano.	1450	Antonelli di Messina. History.	Venice and Florence.
Andrea del Castagna, of Florence.	1410 1480	Dominico Venetiano and Masaccio. History.	Florence, where in the Hall of Justice he painted the Execution of the Conspirators against the House of Medici.

Masters, and their Countries.	Born, Died.	Whose Disciples, and in what they excelled.	Places of Residence, and principal Works.
Cosmo Roselli, of Florence.	1416 1484	History.	Rome and Florence.
Masaccio, of Florence.	1417 1443	Masolino. History.	Florence and Rome, Christ healing one possessed in the Temple.
Giovanni Bellini, of Venice.	1419 1509	His Father Giacomo. History, Portraits, and Architecture.	Venice.
Gentile Bellini, of Venice.	1420 1501	His Father Giacomo. History, Portraits, and Architecture.	Venice and Constantinople.
Leon Battista Alberti, of Florence.	Flo. 1450	Architecture and Sculpture.	Florence, his Books of Architecture, &c.
Antonio Pollaiolo, of Florence, near whose Time the Art of Engraving was found out by Maso Finiguerra, a Goldsmith of Florence.	1426 1498	Andrea del Castagna. History, Architecture, and Engraving.	Florence; his Battle at Florence, engraved on Pewter, with this Inscription, Opus Antonii Pollaiolo Florentini, is said to have been seen by Mantegna, before he did his Triumphs.

Filippino Lippi, of Florence.	1428 1505	His Father Filippo Lippi and Sandro Botticello. History.	Florence and Rome.
Domenico Ghirlandaio, of Florence.	1430 1493	Alesso Baldovinetti. History.	Florence.
Dominico Venetiano, of Venice.	Flo. 1450	Antonello da Messina. History.	Venice and Florence; to the last he brought the Art of Painting in Oil.
Andrea Mantegna, of Mantua.	1431 1517	Jacopo Squarcione. History and Portraits?	Rome and Mantua; his Triumphs of Julius Cæsar, (now at Hampton-Court) which he engraved on nine Plates.
Andrea Verocchio, of Florence, Brother of Antonio.	1432 1488	History and Sculpture.	Florence and Venite; he was the first that found out the Way of taking off a Likeness in Plaister of Paris.
Pietro Pollaiolo, of Florence.	1433 1498	Andrea del Castagna and his Brother. History and Sculpture.	Florence.
Sandro Botticella, of Florence.	1437 1515	Filippino Lippi. History.	Florence.

K 4

Masters, and their Countries.	Born, Died.	Whole Disciples, and in what they excelled.	Places of Residence, and principal Works.
Luca Signorelli, of Cortona.	1439 1521	Pietro del Borgo. History and Naked Figures.	Rome, Cortona, &c.
Pietro di Cosmo, of Florence.	1441 1521	Cosmo Rosselli. History.	Rome.
Bramante Lazari da Urbino.	1444 1514	History and Architecture.	Milan.
Leonardo da Vinci, of a Castle near Florence.	1445 1520	Andrea Verocchio. History, Portraits, and Architecture.	Florence and Milan; at the last is his celebrated Piece of the last Supper.
Gio. Francisco Russico, called Rustichino, of Florence.	Nat. 1446	Andrea Verocchio. History and Sculpture.	Florence.
Pietro Perugino, of Perousa.	1446 1524	Andrea Verocchio. History.	Rome and Florence.
Francisco Raibolini, called Francia, of Bologna.	1450 1526	Marco Zoppo. History.	Bologna; his St. Sebastian was the Study of all the succeeding Bolognian Painters.
Marco Zoppo, of Bologna.	1451 1517	Andrea Mantegna. History.	Bologna.

Name	Nat.		Subject	Place
Gio. Sancio D'Urbino, Father of Raffaele.	1453		History.	Urbin.
Andrea Contucci, called (da Monte) Sanfovino.	1460	1529	Ant. and Pietro Pollaiolo. History.	Florence and Arezzo.
Raffaelino del Garbo, of Florence.	1461	1524	Filippino. History and Portraits.	Florence.
Bernardino Pinturiccio, of Perousa.	1466	1523	Pietro Perugino. History.	Florence and Siena.
Fra. Bartolomeo di S. Marco, of Savignano.	1469	1517	Cosmo Roffelli. History and Portraits.	Florence, he invented the Layman.
Timoteo Vite da Urbino.	1470	1524	Francisco Francia. History.	Bologna and Rome.
Albert Durer, of Nuremberg.	1471	1528	His Father and Michael Wolgemuth. History, Portraits, and Sculpture.	Nuremberg, Inventor of cutting in Wood; his St. Jerome is much esteemed.
Michael Angelo Buonaroti, a Florentine.	1474	1564	Dom. Ghirlandaio. History, Sculpture, and Architecture.	Florence and Rome, where in the Chapple of the Vatican, is his celebrated Piece of the last Judgment.

K 5

Masters, and their Countries.	Born, Died.	Whole Disciples, and in what they excelled.	Places of Residence, and principal Works.
Girolamo Genga D'Urbino.	1476 1551	Pietro Perugino. History & Architecture.	Rome and Florence.
Giorgio del Castel-Franco, called Giorgione.	1477 1511	Gio. Bellino. History and Portraits.	Venice, where is his Christ carrying the Crofs.
Titiano Vecellio da Cadore.	1477 1576	Gio. Bellino and Gorgione. History, Portraits, and Landskips.	Venice, where in Publick are above 50 of his grand Pieces to be seen; he was particularly famous for his Colouring.
Andrea del Sarto, of Florence.	1478 1520	Pietro di Cosmo. History.	Florence; he copied, after Raffaele, Pope Leo X. with such Exactness, as to deceive Julio Romano, who painted the Drapery.
Pellegrino da Modena.	Flo. 1520	Raffaele D'Urbino. History.	Rome and Modena.
Giovanni Antonio da Vezelli, called Sodoma, from his	1479 1554	Naked Figures.	Rome.

Painter			
Baldaſſarro Perucci da Siena.	1481 1536	Hiſtory & Architecture.	Rome; he was the firſt who painted Scenes for the Theatre.
Benevenuti Garofalo, of Ferrara.	1481 1550	Titiano. Hiſtory.	Rome and Ferrara.
Raffaele Sancio D'Urbino, Prince of the modern Painters.	1483 1520	Giovanni his Father, and Pietro Perugino. Hiſtory.	Rome and Florence; his Cartoons at Hampton-Court.
Domenico Becafumi, called Mecarino da Siena.	1484 1549	Pietro Perugino. Hiſtory and Sculpture.	Rome, Siena, and Genoa.
Giov. Antonio Licinio, or Regillo, da Pordodone.	1484 1540	Pellegrino. Hiſtory.	Venice, Mantua, and Ferrara.
Franco Sebaſtiano del Piombo, of Venice.	1485 1547	Gio. Bellino. Hiſtory.	Rome and Venice; at the firſt is his Piece of the raiſing of Lazarus.
Baccio Bandinelli, of Florence.	1487 1559	Gio. Franc. Ruſtico. Hiſtory and Sculpture.	Rome and Florence.
Gio. Franceſco Penni, called Il Fattore di Raffaele, a Florentine.	1488 1528	Raffaele. Hiſtory and Landſkips.	Rome and Naples.
L'Abbate Franceſco Primaticcio, of Bologna.	1490 1570	Giulio Romano. Hiſtory & Architecture.	Bologna, Mantua, &c.

Masters, and their Countries.	Born, Died.	Whose Disciples, and in what they excelled.	Places of Residence, and principal Works.
Polidore da Caravaggio.	1492 1543	Raffaele. History & Architecture.	Rome, Naples, and Messina.
Giulio Romano.	1492 1546	Raffaele. History & Architecture.	Rome and Mantua.
Maturino, of Florence.	1492 1527	Raffaele. History.	Rome.
Jacopo Caruci da Pontormo.	1493 1556	L. da Vinci and A. del Sarto. History and Portraits.	Florence.
Pirro Ligorio, of Naples.	1493 1573	Giulio Romano. History & Architecture.	Naples and Rome.
Antonio Allegri da Correggio.	1494 1534	Mantegna. History.	Modena and Parma.
Giovanni D'Udine.	1494 1564	Giorgione and Raffaele. Ornaments in Stucco.	Rome and Florence; he revived Stucco-work, in Use among the ancient Romans.
Lucas van Leyden, a Dutchman.	1494 1533	Corn. Engelbert. History and Portraits.	Holland, where his Bag-piper (a Print) has been sold for sixty Ducatoons.

	Ob.		
Rogero Bruxellensis, or Roger vander Weyde, of Brussels.	Ob. 1529	History.	Brussels, where in the Hall of Justice he painted those memorable Representations.
John Mabuse, an Hungarian.	Ob. 1532	History and Portraits.	Holland.
John Scborel, a Dutchman.	1495 1562	John Mabuse. History.	Rome, Venice, and Utrecht.
Rosso, of Florence.	1496 1541	Studied Michael Angelo. History.	Italy and France; where in the Palace of Fontainbleau he did the History of Alexander, in 24 Pieces.
Michaele Coxie, of Malines.	1497 1592	Rogero Bruxellensis. History.	Italy and Holland.
Martin Hemskerck, a Dutch-man.	1498 1574	John Scborel. History.	Holland.
Dominico Giulio Clovio, a Sclavonian.	1498 1578	Giulio Romano. History and Portraits, in Miniature.	Rome.
Baittista Franco, called Il Semolei, a Venetian.	1498 1561	Michael Angelo. History.	Rome, Florence, and Venice.

Masters, and their Countries.	Born, Died.	Whose Disciples, and in what they excelled.	Places of Residence, and principal Works.
Hans Holbein, of *Basil*.	1498 1554	His Father. History and Portraits.	*Basil* and *London*; he painted all his Works with his left Hand.
Quintin Matsys, of *Antwerp*.	Ob. 1529	History and Portraits.	*Antwerp*; he was first a Smith, and took to Painting through Love.
Perino del Vaga, of *Florence*.	1500 1547	*Andrea de Ceri*, and *Ridolfi del Ghirlandaio*. History and Architecture.	*Rome*, *Genoa*, and *Pisa*.
Ugo da Carpi.	Flo. 1500	Cutting in Wood.	Found out the Art of Printing in *Chiaro-Scuro*, with three Plates, to imitate Drawings.
John Cornelius Vermeyen, a Dutchman.	1500 1559	History.	*Brussels*; his Beard was so long as to touch the Ground when he stood upright.
John Maio, of *Beverwyck*.	1500 1559	History and Battles.	*Brussels*.

	Flo. / Nat.		
Joachim Patinier, of Dinant in Flanders.		Landskips.	Antwerp.
Gerolamo da Carpi.	1520 1500	Benevenuto Garofalo. History.	Ferrara and Bologna.
Lamberto Lombardo, of Liege, called Suavius.	1556 Nat. 1500	History.	Holland.
Francesco Mazzuoli, called Parmegiano, of Parma.	1504	History and Portraits.	Parma; he invented Etching.
Giacomo Palma, called Palma Vecchio, a Venetian.	1540 1508 1556	Titian. History and Portraits.	Rome and Venice; at the last is his St. Barbara.
Daniele Ricciarelli da Volterra.	1509 1566	Baldassar Peruzzi. History and Sculpture.	Rome and Florence; at the first is his famous Descent from the Cross; it was he who covered the Nudities in Mich. Angelo's Last Judgment.
Francesco Salviati, or Francesco de Rossi, of Florence.	1510 1563	And. del Sarto and Baccio Bandinelli. History and Portraits.	Rome and Florence.
Giacomo da Ponte da Bassano, il Vecchio.	1510 1592	Bonifacio. History, Portraits, and Landskips.	Bassano and Venice.

Masters, and their Countries.	Born, Died.	Whose Disciples, and in what they excelled.	Places of Residence, and principal Works.
Giorgio Vasari Aretino, of Arezzo.	1511 1574	Andrea del Sarto, and Michael Angelo. History, Portraits, and Architecture.	Rome, &c. He writ the Lives of the Painters, in 3 Volumes 4to.
Lelio Urso da Novellara.	1511 1587 Nat.	Michael Angelo. History. Raffaele.	Rome.
Pellegrino da Modena.	1511	History.	Rome and Modena.
Nic. Circiniano, called Pomaranci Vecchio, a Florentine.	1512 1612	History.	Florence.
Giacomo Robusti, called Tintoretto, of Venice.	1512 1594	Titian. History and Portraits.	Venice.
Paris Bordone, a Venetian.	1513 1588	Titian. History and Portraits.	Venice and France.
Gioseppe Porta, or Salviati, a Venetian.	1515 1565	Francesco Salviati. History.	Venice.
Taddeo Zuccaro, of St. Angola in Vado.	1519 1566	His Father. History.	Rome, &c.

Sir *Anthony More*, of *Utrecht*.	1519 1575	*Schoorel*. History and Portraits.	*Flanders, Italy,* &c.
Francis Floris, of *Antwerp*.	1520 1570	*Lambert Lombard*. History.	*Antwerp*, &c.
Paolo Farinato, of *Verona*.	1522 1606	*Nicolo Golfino*. History & Architecture.	*Verona*.
Pelegrino Tibaldi, of *Bologna*.	1522 1592	*Daniele da Volterra*. History & Architecture.	*Bologn, Rome,* and *Milan*.
Andrea Schiavone.	1522 1582	Imitated *Parmegiano, Titian*, &c. History.	*Venice*.
Gregorio Pagani, of *Florence*.	1525 1605	*Maturino* and *Polidoro*. History.	*Florence*.
Luca Cambiagio, of *Genoa*.	1527 1583	*Gio. Cambiagio* his Father. History.	*Genoa*; he painted with both Hands.
Gerolamo Mutiano da Brescia.	1527 1592	*Moretto di Brescia*. History and Landskips.	*Rome*, where he induced Pope *Gregory* XIII. to found the Academy of Painting.
Giovanni Strradano, of *Bruges*,	1527 1604	*Vasario*. History and Hunting-Pieces.	*Florence* and *Bruges*.

Masters, and their Countries.	Born, Died.	Whose Disciples, and in what they excelled.	Places of Residence, and principal Works.
Frederico Barocci, of Urbin.	1528 1612	Battista Venetiano. Religious Subjects.	Urbin and Rome.
Bartolemeo Passerotti, of Bologna.	Nat. 1530	Taddeo Zuccaro. History and Portraits.	Rome.
Paolo Caliari Veronese, of Verona.	1532 1588	Antonio Badile. History and Portraits.	Rome and Venice.
Hans Bol, of Mechlin.	1534 1593	Miniature.	Heidelberg and Amsterdam.
Dieteric Barent, of Amsterdam.	1534 1582	Titian. History and Portraits.	Venice and Amsterdam.
Antony de Montfort Brocklandt, a Dutchman.	1535 1583	Francis Floris. History and Portraits.	Leyden and Amsterdam; at which last is his History of Joseph, much esteemed.
John Calker, or De Calcar, of the Village where he was born, in the Dutchy of Cleves.	Nat. 1536	Titian. History and Anatomy.	Venice; he designed the Anatomy Figures in Vesalius, and the Heads of the Painters in Vasarius.

Cornelius Cort, of Horn.	1536 1578	Engraving History.	Rome and Venice.
Archangelo Salimbeni, of Siena.	1536 1583	History.	Siena.
Giov. Paolo Lomazzo, of Milan.	Nat. 1538	History.	Milan; he wrote 7 Books of the Art of Painting.
Benedetto Caliari, of Verona.	1538 1598	Paul Veronese his Brother. History and Sculpture.	Rome and Venice.
Charles van Mander, a Dutchman.	1539 1607	Lucas de Heer. History.	Rome, Vienna, and Haerlem; he wrote the Lives of the Flemish Painters.
Frederico Zucchero, of Urbin.	1540 1609	Taddeo his Brother. History and Portraits.	Rome, France, &c. He was chosen the first Prince of the Academy of Painting at Rome.
Francisco Bassano.	1540 1594	His Father Giacomo. History. Peter Cock.	Venice.
Peter Breugel, called Old Breugel, a Dutchman.	Flo. 1566	Grotesques and Land-skips, with small Figures.	Antwerp.

Masters, and their Countries.	Born, Died.	Whose Disciples, and in what they excelled.	Places of Residence, and principal Works.
Alexander Casolan, of Siena.	1542 1596	History.	Siena; where in the Church of St. Francis, is a dead Christ, by him.
Martin de Vos, of Parma.	1542 1604	History.	Antwerp.
Bartholomew Spranger, of Antwerp.	Nat. 1546	History.	Rome, Vienna, Antwerp, &c.
Dionisio Calvart, a Fleming.	1547	Prosp. Fontana. History.	Antwerp.
Nicholas Hilliard.	1547	Portraits in Miniature.	London.
Vespasiano Strada;	1547	History.	Rome.
Matthew Brill, of Antwerp.	1550 1584	History and Landskips.	Rome and Antwerp.
John Sadeler, of Brussels.	1550 1600	Engraving History.	Venice, Franckfort, &c.

Giacomo Palma, jun. of Venice.	1551 1628 Nat.	His Father Antony. History.	Venice and Rome.
Roland Savery, of Flanders.	1551	Landskips.	Utrecht, &c.
Cherubino Alberti.	1552 1615	His Father. History and Engraving.	Rome.
Raffaele da Reggio, of Modena.	1552 1580	Fed. Zucchero. History and Landskips.	Rome and Antwerp.
Paul Bril, of Antwerp.	1553 1626	His Brother Matthew. History and Landskips.	Rome; where is his famous Piece of St. Clement, 68 Feet long.
Lodovico Caracci, of Bologna.	1555 1619 Nat.	Prosp. Fontana. History.	Rome and Bologna.
Raphael Sadeler, of Brussels.	1555	Engraving History.	Venice.
Antonio Tempesta, of Florence.	1555 1630	John Strada. Battles, Hunting, &c.	Rome.
Otho Venius, a Dutchman.	1556 1634	Fed. Zucchero. History and Portraits.	Rome, Antwerp, and Brussels.
Giulio Cesare Procaccini, of Bologna.	1556 1634	His Father Ercole. History and Sculpture.	Rome, Venice, Modena, &c.

Masters, and their Countries.	Born, Died.	Whose Disciples, and in what they excelled.	Places of Residence, and principal Works.
Adam van Ort, of Antwerp.	1557 1641	His Father Lambert. History.	Antwerp.
Augostino Carracci, of Bologna.	1557 1602	Dom. Tibaldi. History and Engraving.	Rome, Parma, &c.
Henry Goltius, of Mulbrec.	1558 1617	History and Engraving.	Rome, Naples, and Haerlem.
Jacob Burel, of Blois.	Nat. 1558	Fed. Zucchero. History.	Rome and Paris; where in the Church of the Augustins, is his Descent of the Holy Ghost, which, in the Judgment of Poussin, excells all the Pieces in this City.
Cav. Dom. Passignano, of Florence.	1559 1639	Fed. Zucchero. History.	Florence.
Lodovico Cigoli, of Florence.	1559 1613	History.	Rome and Florence.
Antibale Carracci, of Bologna.	1560 1609	Lod. Carracci. History.	Rome and Bologna.

Cav. *Gioseppe Cesare d'Arpino*, called *Gioseppino*, of *Naples*.	1560 1640	History.	*Rome, Naples*, &c. His most esteemed Pieces are his Battles, in the *Vatican*.
Mark Garrard, of *Bruges*.	1561 1635	History and Portraits.	*London*.
Cornelius Danckeris de Ry, of *Amsterdam*.	1561 1634	Architecture.	*Amsterdam*.
Cav. *Francesco Vanni*, of *Siena*.	1563 1610	*Archangelo Salembeni*. History and Religious Subjects.	*Rome* and *Siena*; in the *Vatican* is his famous Piece of the Fall of *Simon Magus*.
Oratio Gentileschi, of *Pisa*.	1563 1647	*Aurelio Lomi*. History, large.	*Rome, Florence, London*, &c.
Hans Rottenbamer, of *Munich*.	1564 1604	*Tintoret*. History, small.	*Venice* and *Bavaria*.
Henry de Keyser, of *Utrecht*.	1565 1621	Architecture and Sculpture.	*Amsterdam* and *Delft*, where he built that magnificent Tomb of the Prince of *Orange*.
Toby Verhaecht, of *Antwerp*.	1566 1631	Landskips.	*Antwerp*.

Masters, and their Countries.	Born, Died.	Whose Disciples, and in what they excelled.	Places of Residence; and principal Works.
Henry Cornelius Vroom, a Dutchman.	Nat. 1566	Paul Brill. Views and Sea-Pieces.	Venice, Haerlem, &c. He did the famous Sea-fight between the English and Spaniards, in 1588, whence the Tapestry in the Parliament-house was wove.
Abraham Blomaert, of Gorcum.	1567 1647	History.	Utrecht.
Martin Friminet, of Paris.	1567 1619	History.	Rome and Paris.
Steffanino della Bella, of Florence.	1568 1664	Landskips and Cattle.	Florence.
Jan Brueghel, called Velvet Brueghel, of Brussels.	1569 1625	Pet. Goe-kindt. Landskips, Fairs, &c. small.	Brussels.
Michael Angelo Amerigi da Caravaggio.	1569 1609	Cav. Gioseppino. History.	Rome, Venice, &c.
James Matham, of Haerlem.	1571 1631	Hen. Goltius. Engraving History.	Haerlem.

	Nat.		
Ventura Salimbini, of Siena.	1573	His Father Arcangelo. History.	Rome, Siena, &c.
Henry Hondius, of Duffell.	1573	Designing and Engraving, History and Maps.	Hague.
Adam Elsheimer, of Frankfort.	1574 1610	Philip Uffenbach. History and Night-Pieces.	Rome.
Guido Reni, of Bologna.	1575 1643	Denis Calvert. History.	Rome and Bologna.
Gio. Battista Viola, of Bologna.	1575 1622	Hannibal Caracci. History and Landskips.	Rome, &c.
Marcello Provenzale, da Cento.	1575 1639	Paulo Rossetti. History and Mosaic.	Rome; where in the Palazzo Borghese, is the Portrait of Paul V. in Mosaic, wrought with exquisite Art and Judgment.
Sir Peter Paul Rubens, of Cologn, Prince of the Flemish Masters.	1577 1640	Adam van Ort, and Otho Venius. History and Portraits.	Antwerp, Italy, England, and France; the Ceiling of the Banqueting-House at Whitehall, and the Luxemburgh Galleries at Paris, are most admired by the Curious.

L

Masters, and their Countries.	Born, Died.	Whose Disciples, and in what they excelled.	Places of Residence, and principal Works.
Francesco Albano, of Bologna.	1578 1660	D. Calvert and Guido. History.	Rome and Bologna.
Domenico Fetti.	1580 1624	Lodovico Civoli. History.	Rome, Mantua, and Venice.
Jacques Fonquierre, of Antwerp.	1580 1658	Jan Breugel. Landskips.	Antwerp, Paris, &c.
Domenico Zampieri, called Dominichino, of Bologna.	1581 1641	Denis Calvert. History.	Rome, Naples, and Bologna; at the first of which Places is his celebrated Piece of the Communion of St. Jerome.
Cav. Giov. Lanfranco, of Parma.	1581 1647	The Carraches. History.	Rome, Naples, and Parma.
Simon Vouet, of Paris.	1582 1641	His Father. History.	Rome, Venice, and Paris.
Antonio-Caracci, called Il Gobbo.	1583 1618	Hannibal his Uncle. History.	Rome.
Henry Vander Borcht, of Brussels.	Nat. 1583	History.	Italy, Germany, and England.

Name	Dates	Subject	Places
Peter van Laer, called Bamboccio of Haerlem.	1584 1644	History and Landskips.	Haerlem and Amsterdam.
William Nieulant, of Antwerp.	1584 1635	*Roland Savery.* Landskips and Ruins.	Rome, Antwerp and Amsterdam.
James Callot, of Nancy.	1586 1635	Engraving small Figures.	Florence ; his Fair at this Place is a most curious Performance.
Cornelius Poelenburgh, of Utrecht.	1586 1660	*Abraham Blomaert.* Naked Figures and Landskips.	Utrecht, Rome, and London.
Cav. Gio. Francesco Barbieri da Cento, called Guercino, born near Bologna.	1590 1667	*Benedetto Gennari.* History.	Rome and Bologna.
Cornelius Johnson, of Amsterdam.	Flo. 1620	Portraits.	Amsterdam and London.
Gerard Segers, of Antwerp.	1591 1651	*Abraham Janssens.* History.	Antwerp and Madrid.
Gerard Honthorst, of Utrecht.	Nat. 1592	*Abraham Blomaert.* History and Night-Pieces.	Antwerp, London, &c.
Sir Balthazar Gerbier, of Antwerp.	1592	Miniatures in Water-Colours.	Antwerp and London.

L 2

Masters, and their Countries.	Born, Died.	Whose Disciples, and in what they excelled.	Places of Residence, and principal Works.
James Jordaens, of Antwerp.	1594 1678	Adam van Ort. History.	Antwerp.
Nicolas Poussin, of Audley, the Raphael of France.	1594 1665	History and Landskips.	Rome.
Pietro Berrentini da Cortona.	1596 1669	Baccio Ciarpi. History, Sculpture, and Architecture.	Rome and Florence.
Jaques Stella, of Lyons.	1596 1647	History.	Rome, Florence, and Paris.
Cav. Gio. Lorenzo Bernini, of Naples.	1598 1680	History, Sculpture, and Architecture.	Rome and Paris.
Sir Antony Van-Dyck, of Antwerp.	1599 1641	Rubens. History and Portraits.	Antwerp, London, &c.
Viviano Codazzo, called Viviano delle Prospettive, of Bergamo.	1599 1674	Augustino Tasso. Buildings and Ruins.	Rome.
Mario Nuzzi, called Mario dai Fiori, of Orta.	1599 1672	Tomaso Salini his Uncle. Flowers.	Rome.

Name	Dates	Master / Subject	Place
Claudio Gille, of Loraine.	1600 1682	Augustino Tasso. History and Landskips.	Rome.
Jacques Blanchart, of Paris.	Nat. 1600	Nic. Bullery, his Uncle. History.	Rome, Venice, Lyons, and Paris, where, in the Church of Notre-Dame, is his Descent of the Holy Ghost, which they esteem one of their finest Pieces.
Gasparo Dughet, called Gasparo Poussin, of Rome.	1600 1663	Nicolas Poussin. Landskips.	Rome.
Michael Angelo Cerquozzi, called Dalle Battaglie, of Rome.	1600 1660	Antonio Salvatti. Battles and Fruit.	Rome.
Daniel Segbers, the Jesuit, of Antwerp.	1600 1660 Flo.	Jan Breugel. Flowers.	Antwerp.
John Hoskins.	1630	Portraits in Miniature.	London.
Francis de Cleyn, a Dutchman.	1630	History.	Mortlack.
Will. Vande-Velde, called Old Vande-Velde, of Amsterdam.	1670	Sea-Pieces.	Holland and England.

Masters, and their Countries.	Born, Died.	Whose Disciples, and in what they excelled.	Places of Residence, and principal Works.
Andrea Sacchi, of *Rome.*	1601 1661	Cav. Giosepino. History & Architecture.	*Rome.*
Philip de Champagne, of *Bruffels.*	1602 1674 Nat.	History and Portraits.	*Paris.*
Francis Perrier, of *Bourgogne.*	1603	History and Etching.	*Rome* and *Paris.*
Nicolas Mignard, of *Troyes.*	1604 1668	History.	*Rome* and *Paris.*
Padre Giacomo Cortese, called Borgognone, of his Country.	1605 1680	Battles.	*Rome.*
Rembrandt van Ryn, of a Village near Leyden.	1606 1668	Lasman. History and Portraits.	*Amsterdam.*
Wenceslaus Hollar, of *Prague.*	1607 1650 Nat.	Etching Beasts, &c.	*Antwerp, London,* &c.
Abraham Diepenbeck, of *Bois-le-duc.*	1608	Rubens. History.	*Antwerp.*
Adrian Brouwer, of *Haerlem.*	1608 1638	Francis Hals. Drolling-Pieces.	*Antwerp.*

Name	Master / Subject	Dates	Place
Pier-Francesco Mola, of Lugano.	Albani. History.	1609 1665	Rome.
Samuel Cooper, of London.	John Hoskins his Uncle. Portraits in Miniature.	1609 1672	London.
William Dobson, of London.	Portraits.	1610	London and Oxford.
Michael Angelo Pace, called Di Campidoglio.	Fioravanti. Fruits and Still-life.	1647 1610	Rome.
Charles Alphonse du Fresnoy, of Paris.	Perrier and Voet. History.	1670 1611 1665	Rome.
Pietro Testa, of Lucca.	Dominichino and Peter da Cortona. History.	1611 1650	Rome.
Gio. Francesco Romanelli, of Viterbo.	Pietra da Cortona. History.	1612 1662	Rome.
Salvator Rosa, of Naples.	Daniele Falconi. History and Landskips.	1614 1673	Rome.
Michael Dorigny, of St. Quintin.	Vouet. History and Etching.	1616 1665	Paris.
Carlo Dolci, called Carlino, of Florence.	Jacopo Vignali. History.	1616, 1694	Florence.

Masters, and their Countries.	Born, Died.	Whose Disciples, and in what they excelled.	Places of Residence, and principal Works.
Sir Peter Lely, of *Westphalia.*	1617 1680	*De Grebber.* Portraits.	*London.*
Eustache Le Sueur, of *Paris.*	1617 1655	*Vouet.* History.	*Paris.*
Sebastian Bourdon, of *Montpellier.*	1619 1673	History and Landskips.	*France and Sweden.*
Charles le Brun, of *Paris.*	1620 1690	*Simon Vouet.* History and Portraits.	*Rome and Paris.*
Fillippo Lauro, of *Rome.*	1623 1694	*Angelo Carofello.* History in small.	*Rome.*
Carlo Maratti, of *Camorano.*	1625 1713	*Andrea Sacchi.* History and Portraits.	*Rome.*
Luca Giordano, of *Naples.*	1628 1704	*Spagnolet* and *Da Cortona.* History.	*Rome, Naples,* &c.
Ciro Ferri, of *Rome.*	1628 1690	*Peter Da Cortona.* History & Architecture.	*Rome.*
Francis Barlow, of *Lincolnshire.*	1630 1702	Birds and Beasts.	*London.*

Name	Date	Subject	Notes
Sir *Christopher Wren*.	1631 1722	Architecture.	*London*; where he built several Churches, and the Cathedral of St. *Paul*.
Will. Vande-Velde, jun.	1633 1707	His Father. Sea-Pieces.	*London*.
Francis Vander-Meulen, of *Bruſſels*.	1634 1690	History and Views.	*Bruſſels* and *Paris*.
Iſaac Fuller.	Ob. 1676	*Fran. Perrier*. History.	*London* and *Oxford*; at the laſt the Reſurrection in *All-Souls* Chapel is much eſteemed.
Henry Cook.	1642 1700	History.	*London, Oxford,* &c.
John Riley, of *London*.	1646 1691	*Zouſt* and *Fuller*. Portraits.	*London*.
Sir *Godfrey Kneller*.	1646 1723	Portraits.	*London*.
Gioſeppe Paſſari.	1654 1714	*Carlo Maratti*. History.	*Rome*.
Sir *James Thornhill*, the *Engliſh Raphael*.	1677 1734	History.	*London, Oxford,* &c. the Cupola of St. *Paul's, Greenwich* Hoſpital.

L 5

AN

Alphabetical INDEX

OF THE

Chriſtian Names and Surnames of the ENGRAVERS and PAINTERS, with their Places of Abode, and when they flouriſhed, *&c.*

A.

ABbot Primaticcio, *uſed the following Marks*, A. P. M. A. *or* B. *or* Fr. Bol. *or* F. P. *See Number* 91.

A. Blotholinus.

Abraham Bloemaert, Ab. Bl. *he died in* 1647, *aged* 94.

Adam Ælſheimer, *born in* 1574. *See Number* 123.

Adam Mantovano. *Number* 92.

A. D. Bruin. *Number* 20. *flor. in* 1579.

Adrian Collaert. *Number* 22.

Adrian Hubert. *Number* 144.

Agnes Frey, *Wife of* Albert Durer. *Number* 154. *She lived in* 1510.

Agoſtino

Agoftino Parifino. *Number* 57.

Auguftin Carracci, A. C. *or* Agos. C. *of* Bologna, *died in* 1602, *aged* 45.

Auguftin. Metelli, *a Painter of* Bologna. *He died in* 1660.

Auguftin Veneziano, *or* A. V. *flor. in* 1525. *Number* 135.

Albert Aldegraft, *of* Weftphalia, *flor. in* 1551. *Number* 32.

Albert Altorfio, *of* Sweden, *flor. in* 1511.

Albert Clovet, *flor. in* 1675.

Albert Durer, *or* A. E. *of* Nuremberg. *He died in* 1527, *aged* 58. *Number* 30.

Albert Flamen, *flor. in* 1641. *Number* 114.

Albert Golckentonio, A. G.

Alexander Algardi. *He died in* 1654, *aged* 56. *Number* 158.

Alexander Badiali, *of* Bologna, A. B.

Alexander Specchi.

Andrew Andreani, *of* Mantua, *flor. in* 1600. *Number* 47.

Andrew Both, A. Both.

Andrew Camaffei, *a Painter of* Bevagna. *He died in* 1695.

Andrew Laurent, *of* Paris.

Andrew Mantegna, *of* Mantua. *He died in* 1517.

Andrew Salmincio, *of* Bologna, *flor. in* 1640. *Number* 139.

Andrew Vande Venne, *flor. in* 1662. *Number* 151.

Andrew

Bartholomew

Bartholomew Boham, B. B. *of* Nuremberg, *flor. in* 1531.

Bartholomew Chilian, *or* Kilian, *of* Augfburg, *flor. in* 1683.

Bartholomew Coriolano, *of* Bologna, B. C.
Equ. *flor. in* 1640.

Bartholomew Gagliardi. *He died in* 1620.

Bartholomew Paffarotti, *a Painter of* Bologna, B. P. *died in* 1578.

Bartholomew Schenio, B. S. *of* Bologna.

Baptift Brittiano, *of* Mantua.

Baptift Franco, *of* Venice, *died in* 1561.

Bellange, *a* Frenchman.

Benedict Farjat, *flor. in* 1702.

Bernard Faffaro. *Number* 108.

Bernard Balieu, *flor. in* 1700.

Bernard Caftelli. *Number* 102. *He died
in* 1629.

Bernard Gallo, D. B. *flor. in* 1559.

Bernard Malpucci, B. M. *of* Mantua.

Blodelingus *of* Amfterdam.

Bonafoni: *See* Julius Bonafoni, *flor. in*
1547.

Buonmartino: *See* Ifrael Vanmechelin.

Bernard Baron, *of* London.

C.

Camillo Graffico, *of* Forli.

Camillo Porcaccini. *He died in* 1628.

Camillo Congio, *or* CC. *Number* 102.

Caprarola

Caprarola 1597. *He engraved the Death of Chrift from* Hannibal Carracci, *on Silver, in* Caprarola.

Charles Alet, *flor. in* 1693.

Charles Audran, *of* Paris.

Charles Buffagnotti, *of* Bologna, *flor. in* 1704.

Charles Cefio, *an Engraver.*

Charles Cignani, *a Painter of* Bologna, CC.

Charles David, C. D. F.

Charles de la Hay, *flor. in* 1682.

Charles Maratti, *a Painter, of* Rome, *died in* 1713, *aged* 88.

Charles Saraceni : *He died* 1625.

Cefar Fantetti.

Cherubino Alberti : *He died in* 1615. *Number* 100.

Claudius Audran.

Claudius Mellan, *of* Paris, Cl. Mel. *died in* 1688, *aged* 94.

Claudia Stella, *of* Paris, *flor. in* 1686.

Ciro Ferri, *of* Rome, *he died in* 1690.

Conrad Mayr, *of* Zurich, *died in* 1638, *aged* 33.

Conrad Waumans, *flor. in* 1666.

Cormet. *Number* 23.

Cornelius Berghem, *or* Berchen. *Number* 113.

Cornelius Bleker, *flor. in* 1636. C. Bleker.

Cornelius Bloemaert, C. Blo. *born in* 1603: C. B. *and flor. in* 1665.

Cornelius

Cornelius Bofs, *or* Bus. *Numbers* 48, 54, *and* 130.

Cornelius Cort, *of* Holland, *he died in* 1578, *aged* 42.

Cornelius Gallo, *flor. in* 1649.

Cornelius Heviffen. *Number* 38.

Cornelius Polemburg, *of* Utrecht, C. P. *died in* 1660, *aged* 74. *Number* 119.

Cornelius Sichen. *Number* 17.

Cornelius Vermulen, *flor. in* 1706.

Crefcenzius de Honofri.

Crifpin Paffæus, *or* Paffe, *of* Cologn, *died in* 1626. *Number* 163.

Cuerenhert. *Number* 29.

D.

Daniel Mignot. *Number* 41.

David Hopfer, D. H. *flor. in* 1568.

David Van Boons. *Number* 118.

Diana, *of* Mantua, *fhe lived in* 1566.

Dieterico Mayr, *he died in* 1658, *aged* 87.

Dirich Vander Staren. *Number* 12.

Domenichino, D. *of* Bologna, *died in* 1641, *aged* 60.

Domenic Barriera, *of* Florence. *Number* 147.

Domenic Beccafumi, *he died in* 1549. *Number* 140.

Domenic Campagnola, 1518. *Number* 5.

Domenic degli Ambrogi, *of* Bologna.

Domenic Maria Bonavera, *of* Bologna.

Domenic

Domenic Maria Canuti, *of* Bologna, D. M. C.

Domenic Maria Fontana, *died in* 1607, *aged* 64.

Domenic Tempefta, *of* Florence, *flor. in* 1704, *aged* 62.

Domenic Tibaldi, *of* Bologna, *he died in* 1582, *aged* 42.

E.

Edelink, *of* Paris, *died in* 1707.

Edward Fioletti, *of* Bologna, *flor. in* 1612. *Number* 105.

Elias Hainzelman, *of* Augfburg.

Elizabeth Sirani, *a Paintrefs of* Bologna, *died in* 1664, *aged* 26.

Eneas Vighi, *or* Vico, Æ. E. V. *he lived in* 1550. *Number* 160.

Erhardus, *of* Paris.

Efaias Van-Hulfen, E. V. H.

F.

Fabricius Chiari, *of* Rome, *he died in* 1695.

Frederick Barocci, *of* Urbino, F. B. V. I. *born in* 1528, *died in* 1612, *aged* 84.

Flaminius Torre, *of* Bologna, F. T. F. *he died in* 1661.

Florius Macchi, *of* Bologna, *flor. in* 1600.

Francis Aquila.

Francis Briccio, F. B. *of* Bologna, *flor. in* 1600.

Francefchin

Francefchin Carracci, *of* Bologna, *flor. in* 1622.

Francis de Neve, *of* Antwerp.

Francis de Poilly, *of* Paris. *Number* 142.

Francis Maria Francia, *of* Bologna. *Number* 159, *flor. in* 1704.

Francis Giovane.

Francis Grimaldi, *of* Bologna, *flor. in* 1668.

Francis Guerrieri.

F. L. D. Ciatres.

Fr. Lovemont, *flor. in* 1662.

Francis Mazzola, *of* Parma.

Francis Melloni, *of* Bologna.

Francis Spierre, *of* Nancy, *died in* 1681, *aged* 38.

Francis Steen, *or* Vander Steen, *of* Antwerp.

Francis Stringa, *a Painter of* Modena, *flor. in* 1704.

Francis Tortebat.

Francis Vánni, *a Painter of* Sienna. *He died in the Year* 1610, *aged* 47.

Francis Villamena, *flor. in* 1623, *aged* 60. *Number* 117.

Francis Bonaventuri Bifi, F. B. B. *of* Bologna.

Francis Cauveau, *of* France, *died* 1675. *Number* 73.

Francis Perrier, *of* Burgundy, *flor. in* 1635. *Number* 76.

Francis Terzi, *of* Bergamo.

G. Ga-

G.

Galiot Nardois.

Gafpar Reverdin. *Number* 11.

Gerard Fontana.

Giacinto Giminiani. *Number* 89.

Giles Rouffelet, *flor. in* 1686.

Giles Sadeler. *He died in* 1629, *aged* 59.

Giodoco Aman, *of* Zurich, *flor. in* 1588.

George Chriftofano Eimert, *of* Ratifbon, *flor. in* 1683.

George Ghifi, *of* Mantua. *Number* 93.

George Pens, *of* Nuremberg. *Number* 44.

George Perundt, *born in* Franconia, *died in* 1663, *aged* 60.

Giovachino Bocklaer, *of* Antwerp.

Gobbo de Carracci.

Guido Ruggeri. *Number* 156.

Guido Reni, G. R. *of* Bologna, *died in* 1642, *aged* 68.

H.

Hans (*i. e.* John) Baldungh, *or* Baldvin, *flor. in* 1574. *Number* 36.

Hans Bol, H. B. *of* Mechlin, *flor. in* 1541.

Hans Brefanck. *Number* 33.

Hans Brofamer, *flor. in* 1538. *Number* 36.

Hans Burkmayr, *of* Augfburg, *died in* 1517, *aged* 44. *Number* 30.

Hans Liefrinck, H. L. *Number* 146.

Hans Lutenfach. *Number* 58.

Hans Schauflig. *Number* 1.

Hans

Hans Van Culmack, H. V. C. *flor. in* 1517.

Hannibal Carracci, *a Painter of* Bologna, A. C. P. *died in* 1609.

Henry Bloemaert, *flor. in* 1647.

Henry Cliven, *he died in* 1589. *Numbers* 124. and 152.

Henry Blofeuvertus Frifius.

Henry Goltzius, *of* Holland ; *he died in* 1617, *aged* 59. *Number* 111.

Henry Hondius, *born in* 1573.

Herman Coblent. *Number* 144.

Hercules Bazicaluva, *of* Florence, *flor. in* 1641.

Hercules Septimius, H. S. *or* Hercules Setti, *of* Modena, *flor. in* 1571.

Hifberto Venio.

Hieronymus, *or* Jerome Mocetus. *Number* 13.

Hifbel, *or* Hifbin. *Number* 31.

Hoefnaghel, Joris Hoefnaghel, *a Painter of* Antwerp, *he died in* 1600.

Horace Borgiano, H. B. *of* Piftoia. *Number* 36.

Hiacinth Giminiani. *See* Giacinto.

Hubert Audenaerd.

Hubert Goltzius, *he died about the Year* 1503, *aged* 57.

Hubert Vincentini.

I. James

I.

James Belli, *of* France, I. B. F. *or* Belli fec.

James de Gheyn, *flor. in* 1615, *aged* 50. *Number* 122.

James Mattamius, *of* Haerlem. *He died in* 1631, *aged* 60.

James Sandrart, *of* Nuremberg, *flor. in* 1683.

James Vander Heyden, *of* Augſburg, *flor. in* 1608.

James Lutma, *of* Amſterdam, *flor.* 1681.

James Grand Homme, I. G. Van Ulïet. *Number* 112.

James Kerver, I. K.

James Bink, *of* Nuremberg, 1500. I. B.

James Blondeau, *flor. in* 1690.

James Callot, *of* Lorrain, *he died in* 1635.

James Freij, *of* Rome.

James Laurenzani.

James Lauri.

James Ligozzi.

James Maria Giovannini, *of* Bologna, *he died in* 1717.

James Matham, *of* Holland, *he died in* 1631.

John Chantry, *flor. in* 1662.

Jerome Hopfer, I. H.

J. Blondeau, *that is*, James, *flor. in* 1690.

J. G. Van Uliet: *See* James Grand Homme.

John Covay, *of* France. *Number* 72.

John

John Ladefpeldrickt. *Number* 45.

John le Pautre, *a* Frenchman, *Engraver of divers Subjects.*

J. G. Bronchorft, *i. e.* John, *flor. in* 1662. *Number* 119.

J. Gal. Nardois F. *i. e.* John Galeot Nardois fecit.

John Abach, *born in* Cologn *in* 1556, *flor. in* 1597.

John Baptift Brixianus, J. B. B.

John Baptift Mantuanus, J. B. M. *flor. in* 1500.

John Culembach, *of* Nuremberg, *flor. in* 1512.

John Francus, *of* Augfburg.

John George Walderich, *of* Augfburg.

John James Thourneiffen, *of* Bafil, *flor. in* 1667.

John Livius, J. L. fec.

John (*or* Hans) Sebald Beham, *he died in* 1545. *Number* 31.

John Andrew Podefta, *of* Genoa.

John Andrew Sirani, *of* Bologna.

John Baron, *of* France, *flor. in* 1644.

John Baptift Bolognini, *a Painter of* Bologna.

John Baptift Bonaccini.

John Baptift Caftiglioni. *Number* 95.

John Baptift Conftantini.

John Baptift Coriolani, *an Engraver of* Bologna.

John

John Baptift Falda, *of* Rome.

John Baptift Galleftrucci. *Number* 155.

John Baptift Maggi, *of* Rome, *Painter and Engraver.*

John Baptift, *of* Mantua, *flor. in* 1500.

John Baptift Mercati.

John Baptift Sorito, *flor. in* 1621.

John Baptift Pafqualino, *flor. in* 1622.

John Baptift Ricci, *of* Novara.

John Baptift Teftana.

John Baptift Vanni.

John Baptift Zani, *of* Bologna.

John Benedict Caftiglioni, *of* Genoa. *Number* 95.

John Calcar, *of* Cleves, *he died in* 1546.

John Cæfar Tefta, *Nephew to* Peter Tefta.

John Frederick Greuter, *of* Strafburg.

John Francis Caffioni, *an Engraver in Wood.*

John Francis Venturini.

John Francis Zabello. *Number* 83.

John George Nuvolftella, *a* German, *died in* 1624, *aged* 30.

John Guerra, *of* Modena, *he died about the Year* 1612.

John William Baur. *See* Guil. Baur.

John Jofeph dal Sole, *a Painter of* Bologna, *flor. in* 1704.

John James Coraglio, *of* Verona, *an Imitator of* Marc Antonio Raimondi.

John Lanfranci, *a Painter of* Parma, *died in* 1647, *aged* 66.

John

John Lewis Valefio, *of* Bologna, VAL. *died in* 1643. *Number* 103.
John Lutma, *of* Amfterdam, *flor. in* 1681.
John Maria, *of* Brefcia. *Number* 8.
John Miele, *of* Flanders, *flor. in* 1648.
John Nicola, *of* Venice, *flor. in* 1555.
John Orlandi, *flor. in* 1600.
John Podefta.
John Sadeler, *he died in* 1600, *aged* 58.
John Saenredam, *of* Holland. *Number* 121.
John Schorel, *of* Bavaria, *he died in* 1562, *aged* 67. *Number* 60.
John Trofchel, *of* Nuremberg, *he died in* 1633.
John Viani, *a Painter of* Bologna, *died in* 1700, *aged* 63.
Jofeph Maria Metelli, *flor. in* 1704. *Number* 138.
Jofeph Maria Roli, *of* Bologna, G. M. R.
Jofeph Moretti, *of* Bologna, *an Engraver on Wood and Copper, born* 1657, *flor. in* 1704.
Jofeph Ribera. *Number* 129.
Jofeph Teftana, *flor. in* 1654.
Jofeph Zarlati, *of* Modena.
Joris Hoefnaghel, *fee* Hoefnaghel.
Joft Amon. *Number* 37.
Ifaac Major, *of* Franckfort, *flor. in* 1620.
Ifrael Martino, I. M. *Number* 186.
Ifrael Meck, *or* Van Meck, I. M. *flor. in* 1623.

Ifrael

Ifrael Silveftre, *of* France.

J. Van Velde. *Number* 127.

Julius Bonafoni, J. B. F. *of* Bologna, *flor. in* 1547.

Julius Cæfar Porcaccinus, J. C. Porc. In. *died in* 1626, *aged* 78.

Julius Cæfar Venenti, *of* Bologna. *Number* 137.

Juftus Sadeler, *of* Bruffels, I. S. E. *flor. in* 1620. *Number* 157.

Julius Campagnola, *of* Venice, *flor. in* 1520.

L.

Lambert Lombardo, L. *or* L. L. *or* L. S. *died in* 1560, *aged* 60.

Lambert Suave, *or* Sufterman, *is the same as* Lambert Lombardo.

Lambert Hopfer. *Number* 21.

Leonard Gualtier, *flor. in* 1618. *Number* 70.

Leonard Parafole Norfino, *flor. in* 1600.

Lewis Carracci, L. C. *died in* 1610, *aged* 64.

Lewis Cardi Cigoli, L. C. C. *of* Florence,

Lewis Mattioli, *of* Bologna, *flor. in* 1704.

Lewis Scalzi.

Lawrence Loli, L. L.

Lawrence Tinti, *of* Bologna. *flor. in* 1666.

Louvemont, *flor. in* 1662.

Luke Ciamberlano.

Luke

Luke Cranogio, *or* Van Craen, *or* V. C. *or* L. V. C. *Numbers* 26 *and* 35.

Luke de Leida, *called of* Holland. *Number* 34.

Luke Kilian, *of* Augfburg, *Junior*, *or* L. K. A. *flor. in* 1657.

Luke Kruger, *a* German, *flor. in* 1516.

Luke Penni, *or* Lucas, P. R. *of* Florence, *flor. in* 1528.

Luke Van Uden, L. V. V. *flor. in* 1662, *aged* 67.

Luke Vorfterman, *of* Antwerp, *flor. in* 1629. *Number.* 120.

Lewis Gomie.

Lewis Scaramuccia Perugino, *died in* 1684.

Lewis Philip Boitard, *of* London.

M.

Marc Antonio Chiarini, *of* Bologna.

Marc Antonio Raimondi, *or* M. A. F. *died in* 1528. *Number* 99.

Marc da Ravenna, M. R.

Marottus.

Martin de Clef, M. C. *flor. in* 1436.

Martin de Secu, *or* M. + S. *Number* 39.

Martin de Vos, *of* Antwerp, *a celebrated Inventor for Engravers*, *died in* 1604, *aged* 72.

Martin Hemfkirk, *a principal Inventor for Engravers*, *died in* 1574, *aged* 76. *Number* 24.

Martin Rota, *of* Sabina, *flor. in* 1725. *Number* 109.

Martin Zinkius, *or* Zazingeri, M. Z. *or* Z. A. *flor. in* 1500.

Maſo Finiguerri, *of* Florence, *one of the firſt Engravers on Copper, in* 1460.

Matthew Grunevald, *of* Afchaffemburg. *Numbers* 30, *and* 153.

Matthew Greuter, *of* Straſburg, M. G. *he died in* 1638, *aged* 72.

Matthew Merian, M. Merian, *born in* Barbary, *in* 1593, *and died in* 1632.

Matthew Kuſel, *of* Augſburg.

Matthew Piccioni, *of* La Marca, *flor. in* 1655.

Matthew Zagel, M. Z. *Number* 10.

Maurice Oddi, *died in* 1702, *aged* 63. *Number* 134.

Melchior Girardini, Mel. Gir. Fec. *of* Rome.

Melchior Kuſel, *of* Augſburg, *Brother to* Matthew, *flor. in* 1652.

Melchior Lorichio, M. L.

Micarino. *Number* 9.

Michael L'Aſne, *died in* 1667, *aged* 72. *Number* 75.

Michael Le Blon. *Number* 6.

Michael Angelo Guidi, *Son of* Raphael.

Michael Cocxie, *died in* 1592, *aged* 95. *Number* 3.

Michael Lucchefe. *Number* 107.

Michael

Michael Natali, *of* Lodi, *flor. in* 1665.
Michael Volgemut, *of* Nuremberg, Albert
  Durer's *Mafter, flor. in* 1490.
Mr. Lane.
Mr. Rolet.
Mr. Vanfculp.

N.

Nicholas Vicentino, *he engraved the Works*
  of Parmigiano, *and flor. in* 1555.
Nicholas Chapron, *of* Paris, N. C. *flor. in*
  1649.
Nicholas Manuel, *of* Bearn, N. M. B. *flor.*
  in 1518.
Nicoletto, *of* Modena.
Nicholas Beatricetto.
Nicholas Beatrici, *of* Lorrain, N. B. L. F.
  Number 149.
Nicholas Bylli.
Nicholas de Bruin, N. B.   *Number* 28.
Nicholas du Puys, *of* Paris.
Nicholas Dorigny, *of* Paris.
Nicholas la Fas, *a* Frenchman.
Nicholas Laigniel.
Nicholas Mignard, *of* Paris, *died in* 1695,
  aged 85.
Nicholas Perrelle, *a* Frenchman, *Engraver*
  to Nicholas Pouffin, *and others.*
Nicholas Poilly, *a* Frenchman, *died in*
  1696, *aged* 70.
Noel Garnier, *flor. in* 1618. *Number* 4.

O.

Oliver Gatti, *an Engraver of* Bologna, *flor. in* 1626.
Oliver Dolfin, *he died about* 1693.

P.

Padre Angelo Lorenzini, Min. Conv. Bol.
Paul Brill, *of* Antwerp, *died in* 1626, *aged* 72.
Paul Bianchi, P. B. F.
Paul Pontius, *of* Antwerp, *flor. in* 1660, *aged* 57.
Paul Maupini.
Periecouter. *Number* 40.
Peter Aquila, *flor. in* 1681.
Peter Artfen.
Peter Breughel, *died in* 1556. *Number* 123.
Peter Cottart. *Number* 46.
Peter Daret, *of* Paris, *flor. in* 1654. *Number* 74.
Peter de Jode, *the Elder, born in the Year* 1602, *and died in* 1634.
Peter del Po.
Peter Hys, P. H.
Peter Ifelburgh, *of* Cologn, *flor. in* 1620.
Peter Lombard, *flor. in* 1666. *Number* 71.
Peter Mercand. *Number* 42.
Peter Mignard.
Peter Quaft. *Number* 43.
Peter Ryfbrack, *on his Landfkips.*

Peter

Peter Santi Bartoli, P. SS. Bart. *of* Perugia, *died in* 1700, *aged* 65.

Peter Soutman.

P. Servuter.

Peter Simon, *of* Paris, *flor. in* 1673.

Peter Stefanoni, P. S. f.

Peter Stivens, *of* Mechlin, *flor. in* 1629.

Peter Tefta, *of* Lucca, *he died in* 1651, *aged* 41. *Number* 96.

Peter Vander Borcht, P. V. Borcht.

Peter Vander Nelpe. *Number* 115.

Peter Vanfickleer.

Peter Voeriot. *Number* 53.

Philip Adler, *of* Padua. *Number* 16.

Philip Abiati, *of* Milan, *flor. in* 1704.

Philip Napolitano.

Philip Paffari.

Philip Thommafini, Phil. Th. *flor. in* 1589.

R.

Raphael Guidi, *of* Tufcany.

Raphael Sadeler, *born in* 1555, *and flor. in* 1595.

Raphael Scaminoffi. *Number* 104.

Raphael Sancio, *an Inventor.* *Numbers* 99, *and* 145.

Raymond La Fage.

Ravenftein, *or* Gafpar Reverdin, *flor. in* 1640. *Number* 11.

Rayner

Rayner Perfino, *of* Amfterdam, *a Companion of* Cornelius Bloemaert.

Ravignano, *fee* Mark da Ravenna. R. S.

Regnaffon, N. *flor. in* 1646.

Rembrandt, *or* Van Rhin, *died in* 1668, *aged* 62. *Number* 126.

Remigio Cantagallina.

Reynold Boivin, *alfo* Renato. *Number* 7.

Reynold Lochon. *Number* 69.

Ralph Brein, *of* Zurick.

Ralph Mayr, *flor. in* 1638.

Robert de Vorft, *flor. in* 1628.

Robert Nanteuil, *a* Frenchman, *he died in* 1678, *aged* 48.

Robetta, R. B. T. A.

R. V. A. Gaudenfis.

S.

Saenredam, *See* Hans (*or* John) Saenredam.

Salvator Rofa, *a Painter, Engraver and Poet, of* Naples ; *he died in* 1675, *aged* 60. *Number* 106.

San Martino, *of* Bologna, *this Artift was* Abbot Primaticcio, *of St.* Martin's. *Number* 91.

Samuel Hainzelmanus, *of* Augfburg.

Schelde a Bolfuvert, *flor. in* 1660. *Number* 125.

Scuppen, *of* Paris.

Saben-

Sabenzanus. *Number* 109.
Silveſtre da Romana. *Number* 101.
Simon Cantarini, *called of* Peſaro, S. C.
Simon Friſio.
Simon Guillain, S. G. *of* Paris, *flor. in* 1646.
Simon, *of* Paris, *flor. in* 1673.
Sinibaldo Scorza, *of* Genoa, *he died in* 1631, *aged* 41.
Siſto Badalochio, *of* Parma, *flor. in* 1607.
Spagnoletto, *See* Joſeph Ribera. *Number* 129.
Stephen della Bella, *of* Florence. S. B. *he died in* 1664, *aged* 50. *Number* 136.
Stephen Baudet, *of* France, *flor. in* 1675.
Stephen Carteron, S. C. F. *flor. in* 1615.
Stephen Colbenſtagh, *of* Rome. *Number* 94.
Stephen du Perac, *of* Paris, *he died in* 1601.
Stoltzius. *Number* 2.
Svaneburgh, *he engraved the Works of* Rubens.
Suſanna Sandrart, *of* Norimberg, *flor. in* 1683.

T.

Theodore Cornher, *of* Amſterdam, *he died in* 1590.
Theodore Crugher, *or* Greuger, T. C. *Number* 150.

M 4 Theo-

Wen-

Wenceflaus Hollar, *a* Bohemian, *died in* 1677.

Wolfgangus Kilian, *of* Augfburg, *flor. in* 1654.

W. Vaillant, *flor. in* 1675.

W. Vaillant, *flor. in* 1726.

Z.

Zazingeri, *See* Martin Zinkio.

Zinkio *is the fame as* Martin Zazingeri.

M 5   A N

A N

Alphabetical L I S T

O F T H E

SURNAMES *before the* CHRISTIAN NAMES, *of* Painters, Engravers, *and* Sculptors.

Note, *The Letters* P *and* S, *before the Names, stand for* Painter, *or* Sculptor.

A Back, John
Abiati, Philip
Adamo, Mantuano
Ackerftout, William
Adam, John
Adler, Philip
P. Ælfheimer, Adam
Agoftino, Veneziano
Aguccio, Giovanni
Alberti, Cherubino
Aldegraft, Albert
S. Algardi, Aleffandro
Allard, Carolus
Alet, John Charles

Allen, Francis
Altorf, Adam
Ambrogi, Domenico delli
Ab - Amling, Cornelius, Guftavus
————, Carolus
· Guftavus
Amon, Juftus
P.————, Jodocus
Ammon, Claudius
Andrea, Nicolas
Andreani, Andrea

Angelo, Michael, *see*
Buonaroti
Anrien, J. B. r.
Aquila, Francis
———, Petrus
Artfen, Petrus
Aubry, Peter
Aveline, *fen.*
Audenaerd, Hubert
Audran, Charles
P.———, Gerard
———, Benedict
———, Claude
———, John
Auroux, Nicholas.
B.
*P.*Badaloccio, Sifto
*P.*Badiale, Aleffandro
Baldung, Hans
*P.*Baldini, Baccio
Balieu, Bernard
———, Peter de
*P.*Baltens, Peter
Balthafar, Peter
P. & S. Bandinelli, Baccio
Barbé, John
Barlacchius, Thomas
Baron, John
Baron, Bernard
*P.*Barocci, Frederico
Baroni, Giufeppi
Barri, Giacomo
Barriera, Domenico
*P.*Bartoli, Pietro Santo
Baudet, Eftienne

*P.*Baugin, John
Baumgartner, J. G.
Bary, Henry
*P.*Baur, Guil. *or* Jo.
Will.
*P.*Bazicaluva, Hercules
Bazin, Nicolas
*P.*Beatrici, Nicolas
Beatricetto, Nicolò
Beauvais
*P.*Beccafumi,Domenico
Becket, Ifaac
Beham, John Sebald
Belange
Belli, Jaques
Berghem, Cornelius
*P.*Bernardi, Gio.
Bertrand, Philip
Beaufrere, P.
Beufecom, T. V.
Bertelli, Ferando
———, Lucas
Bettini, Domenico
Beverenfis, Nicafius
Bianchi, Paolo
Bignon, Francis
P. & S. Bink, Jacobus
Bie, Jaques de
Bifcaino, Bartol.
Bifi,Fra. Bonaventura
Blancus, Paulus
Bleker, Cornelius
Blefendorf, Samuel
Blefwart, Henry
Blefwick, F.
*P.*Bloemart, Abraham
Bloemaert,

M 6

Bloemaert, Cornelius
————, Frederick
————, Hercules
Blois, A. de
P.Block, Daniel
P.——, Emanuel
P.——, Adolphus
P.——, Benjamin
Blon, Michael le
Blond, la
Blondeau, Jaques
Bloeteling, A.
Bocklin, J. C.
P.Bocklaer, Joachim
Boel, Quirinus
——, C.
Boham, Bartolomeus
Bois, M. de
Boivin, René
Boiſſavin, L.
Boitard, Lewis Philip
Bol, Hans
P.Bolognese, Francesco,
   See Primaticcio
Bolognini, Jo. Bap-
   tiſt
Bolonnois, E. de
Bolſwaert, Scalfe a
Bolſwerd, Bl.
————, Boetius
Bolzoni, Andrea
Bonaccini, Jo. Bap-
   tiſt
Bonar, A.
Bonaſone, Julio
Bonavera, Domenico

Bonez.
Buonmartino, Iſrael
   Martin
Bonnart, Nicolas
Bonvicinus, B.
Borgiano, Horatio
Borrecheus, Matthew
Bos, *or* Bus, Corne-
   lius
Bos, *or* Boſch
P.Boſs, Antoine
Both, Andrew
Bouché, Pet. Paul
Bouchet
Boulanger, John
Boud, R.
Boudan, L.
Boutatts, John
————, Philip, *jun.*
————, Frederick
————, P. Balthaſar
————, G.
P.Brebiette, Peter
P.Brein, Rodolf
Breſanck, Hans
P.Breſcia, Giov. Maria
   da
————, Giov. An-
   tonio
P.Breughel, Peter
Briſsart, P.
P.Brill, Paul
P.Briſcio, Francesco
Brittiano, Baptiſta
Brixianus, J. Baptiſt

Brixianus,

Brixianus, Jo. Antonio
Bronchorſt, John
Broſamer, Hans
Bruf, John
Brun, G. le
P.———, Charles le
Brun, Horatio
Brun, Peter de
Bruin, A. D.
———, Nic. de
Brye, Theodore de
Buffagnotti, Carlo
P. & S. Buonaroti, Mi. Angelo
P.Burchmair, Hans
Burnford, Thomas
Bylli, Nicolo.

C.

P.Caccianemici, Vincenzo
P. & S. Calcar, John
Callot, Jaques
Camaſſei, Andrea
Campagnola, Domenico
———, Julio
P.Candidus, Peter
Cantagallina, Remigio
Cantarino, Simone
Canuti, Domenico Maria
Capitellus, Bernardus
Capriolo, Aliprando

P.Carracci, Agoſtino
P.———, Annibal
P.———, Antonio
P.———, Franceſco
P.———, Lodovico
P.———, Paolo
Cardi, Lodovico
Carpi, Ugo da
Cars, J. F.
Carteron, Stephanus
Caſſione, J. F.
Caſtelli, Bernardo
Cauſe, Henry
P.Caſtiglione, Jo. Benedict
———, Jo. Baptiſt
P.Ceſio, Carlo
Du Change, G.
Chapron, Nicolas
Chaſteau, N.
Du Chaſtel
Chaveau, Francois
Chatres
Chereau, F.
Cheron, Elizabeth
Cherpinion, C.
Cheſneau, Henry
Chevau, F.
P.Chiari, Fabritio
Chiarini, Marc Antonio
Cignani, Carlo
Ciamberlano, Luca
Ciro, Ferri

P. Clef,

P.Clef,*or*Cliven,Hen.de
P.————, Martin de
P.Clerc, le, *jun.*
————, Sebaſtien
Cloe, Aubert
Clovet, Albert
Clouvet, P.
————, R.
Cluet, Hubert
Coblentz, Herman
Cochin, *ſen.*
————, *jun.*
Cock, Jerom
Coenhert, Theodore
————, Dirich
Coenradt, Lowers
Cocxis, Michael
Coget, Anthony
Cokerken, Cornelius
————, E. van
Colbenſtagh, Stephen
Collaert, Adrian
Collin, Richard
————, Nicolas ·
Congius, Camillo
Conrad, Abraham
Conſtantini, Jo. Baptiſt
Coquin, Lovis
Coraglio, Jo. Jacob
Coricori, Girolamo
Coriolanus, Bartolomeus
Cormet
Cort, Cornelius

Corteſe, William
Coffin, Lovis
Conrad, Abraham
Cottart, Peter
Cotta, Jac.
Couvay, John
Cranogio, Lucas
Cremonius, Andreas
Crepy
Cruger, Theodore
P.Culembach, John
Culot
Cundier, John
Curti, Franceſco
Cuſtodis, Domenico.
D.
Dac, John, *the ſame with* John Aback
Dalla Croce, Theodore
Dankers, Henry
Dankert, Cornelius
Dannoot, Peter
Daret, Peter
David, Jerom
————, Carolus
————, Henry
Delft, William
————, Jacob
Della Bella, Stephano
Del-Pò, Pietro
Derlois, M.
Dertellius, Lucas
Deſrochers, Eſtienne
————, *jun.*
Devaux, Robert
Diamner,

Diamner, H. F.
P. Dolfin, Olivier
Doino, Catterino
P. Domenico, Fiorentino
P. Domenichino, *or* Dom. Zampieri
Dorat, Jac.
Dorigni, Michael
————, Nicolas
Doffier, M.
Drevet, Peter
————, Claude
Dubois, M.
Du Change, Gafpar
Duflos, Claude
Dupuis, Nicolas
————, Fr.

E.

Edelinck, Gerard
————, Nicolas
Eimart, Geo. Chrift.
Eland, Henry
Elipart, J. Ch.
Elftrac, Robert
Erhard
Erlinger, Francis.

F.

Faber, John, *fen.*
————, John, *jun.*
Fage, Nicolas la
Faithorn, William
Falda, Jo. Baptift
Falk, John
————, Jerom

Fantetti, Cefare
Farjat, Benedict
P. Farinati, Paolo
Febure, le
Ferace, Canute
Fevre, Claude le
Filian, John
P. Finiguerra, Mafo
Fiolettus, Edward
Flamen, Albert
Floræ, Guill. Nicolas a
Flos, Claude du
P. Fontana, Dom. Maria
————, Gerardo
P. ————, Veronica
Francia, Francefco Maria
Francoforma
Francus, Baptifta
Freij, Agnes
Freij, Giacomo
Fiizius, Simon
Frofno, John
Fruytiers, Philip.

G.

Gagliardus, Philip
Gagliardi, Bartolomeo
Galle, Theodore
Galle, Philip
————, Cornelius, *fen.*
————, Cornelius, *jun.*
Gallo, Bernardo

Gal-

Galleſtrucci, Jo. Bap-
tiſt
Gantrel, Stephen
Garnier, Noel
Gatti, Oliviero
Gaudenſis, R. V. A.
Gautier, Leonard
Georgi, George
——, John
P.&S. De Ghein, Jaq.
Ghiſi, Georgio
Giffart, Peter
Giminiano, Jacintho
Giovane, Francefco
Giardini, Melchior
Glover, George
Gole, John
Gomie, Luigi
Golkentonius, Al-
bertus
*P.*Goltzius, Hubert
P. ——, Henry
Gourdelle
Graffico, Camillo
Granhomme, Jaques
Greut, Jofeph
Greuter, F.
——, Theodore
P.——, Matthew
P.——, Jo. Frede-
rick
*P.*Gribelin, Sam.*fen.*
——, Sam. *jun.*
Grignon, Jaques
Grimaldi, Francefco
Grunevald, Matthew

Guarnier, Anthony
Guerra, Giovanni
Guerrieri, Francefco
*P.*Guidi, Rafael
——, Mich. Agnolo,
his Son
*P.*Guido Reni
Guignon, V.
Guillain, Simon
Gyger, Jo. Conrad.
H.
Habert, N.
Haelwegh, Albert
Hagen, S.
Hainzelman, John
——, Samuel
Halbeck, John van
Hallé, S.
Hanzelman, Elias
Harrewin
Hay, Charles de la
Hemſkirk, Martin
Heiden, Jacob ab
Heim, W. C.
Heince, Zachary
Hendricx, Giles
Herkenever, Jac.
Guil.
——, Leonard
Herthemels, Maria
Hertz, Jo. Daniel
Heviſſen, Cornelius
Hiſben, Peun
Hoefnaghel, Joris
Hoelwigh, Adrian
Hogenberg
Holbens,

Holbens, *of* Haerlem
Hollar, Wenceſlaus
Holſtein, P.
·P.Hondius, Henry
———, William
Honofri, Creſcenzo
Hopfer, Jerom
———, David
———, Lambert
Houbraken, Jaques
Houget, John
Houſſe, Patil de la
Hubert, Gaſpar
———, Adrian
Huberti, Francis
Hulſius, Francis
Humbelot
Huret, Gregory
Huybreckt, Peter
Hys, Peter.

I.

Jacquart, Ant. de
Jeaurat, E.
Imperiali, Girolamo
Jode, Peter de, *ſen.*
———, Peter de, *jun.*
Jolain, Jac.
Jongelinx, J. B.
———, J. P.
Jongh, J. de
Iſaac
Iſac, Jaſpar
Iſelberg, Peter
Juſter, J.

K.

Kaldung, Hans
Kerver, Jaques
Kilian, Lucas, *ſen.*
———, Lucas, *jun.*
P.———, Bartholomew
———, Wolfgang
———, Philip
Koning, Cornelius
Kraling, John
Kruger, Lucas
Kuſſel, Matthew
———, Melchior.

L.

Ladelſpeldricht, John
Laignel, Nicolas
Lamſweard, Stephen
  van
Landry, P.
Lanferrius, Antonius
Lanfrank, Giovanni
Lang, Mauritz
Langlois, John ·
Larmeſſin, D. de
Laſne, Michael
Later, John de
Lankerken, Corne-
  lius
Laurent, Andrew
Laurentio, Eſaré
Laurenzani, Giaco-
  mo
Lauri, Giacomo
Lawers, Nicolas
Lawers,

Lawers, Conrad
Le Bas, Jaques Phillipe
Lenfant, John
Leonart, G. F.
————, J. F.
*P.*Leonus, Octavius
Lens, Bernard
Leotard
Lepicié
*P.*Leyden, Lucas van
Leyfebetten, P. V.
Licinio, Antonio
Liefrank
Liefrinck, Hans
Lieu, Thomas de
Ligozzi, Giacomo
Lifibet, P.
Lochon, René
*P.*Lolli, Lorenzo
Lombardus, Lambertus
Lombart, Peter
Lommelin, Adrian
————, G.
*P.*Lorenzini, Padre Angelo
Lorichius, Melchior
Louvement, Francis
Louys, John
Lubin, Jaques
Lucchefe, Michael
Luciani, Antonio
Lucini, Ant. Francefco
*P.*Lutma, Janus
Luyken, John

Lyvius, John.
M.
*P.*Macchi, Floria
*P.*Maggi, Jo. Baptift
Magliar, A.
*P.*Major, Ifaac
Malleri, Philip de
————, Charles
Malpucci, Beraio
*P.*Mantegna, Andrea
Mantuana, Diana
Mantuanus, Giorgio
————, Jo. Baptift
Manuel de Berna, Nic.
*P.*Maratti, Carlo
Marc. Ant. Raimondi
Maria, Domenico
Mariette, P.
————, John
Mariotti
Martinez
Martino, Ifrael
Maffon, Antoine
*P.*Matham, Jaques
P.————, Theodore, *his Son*
*P.*Mattioli, Lodovico
Mavelet, Charles
Maupini, Paolo
*P.*Mayer, Dieterick
————, Henry
————, Conrad
P.————, Rodolf
*P.*Mazzola, Francefco
Meck, *or* V. Mechelin, Ifrael
Melar,

Melar, Adrian
Mellan, Claude
Mellan, G.
Melloni, Francesco
Mercand, Pierre
Mercati, Jo. Baptist
Merian, Matthew
Merl, John
Meffager, John
*P.*Metelli, Agostino
P.————, Giof. Maria
Meyffens, John
————, Cornelius
Micarino
*P.*Miele, Giovanni
Mignard, Nicolas
P.————, Pierre
Mignot, Daniel
Mocetus, Hieronymus
Moncornet, B.
Montbard
Moretti, Giufeppi
Morin, John
Moro, Battista del
Moyreau, John
Muller, John
————, Harman
Muckerken.

N.
Nadat
Nantueil, Robert
Napolitano, Filippo
Nardois, J. Galiot
Natalis, Michael
Nefs, Jaques

Neve, Francis
Nicoletto, da Modena
Nuvolftella, Jo. Geo.

O.
Occo, Adolphus
Oddi Parmagiano,
    Mauro
Orlandi, Giovanni
Ottens, F.

P.
Panorn, Alois Calab.
*P.*Paul Veronefe, *or* Ca-
    liari
*P.*Parafole Norfino, Le-
    onardo
P. Parmegiano, Fran-
    cefco ☞
Parmegianino, Fran-
    cefco
Pafquilino, Jo. Bap-
    tift
Pafs, Crifpin, *fen.*
————, Crifpin, *jun.*
————, *or* Paffeus, Si-
    mon
Paffari, Filippo
Paffaro, Bernardino
*P.*Paffarotti, Bartolo-
    meus
Patavinus, Gafpar
————————, Gerard
Patigny
*P.*Pautre, John le
Payn, John
Peel, Matthew
                Penni,

Penni, Lucas
P.Pens, George
P.Peroch, Eftienne
P.Perelle, Nicolas
Periecouter
P.Perrier, Francois
P.Perfin, Rainerus
Perundt, George
P.Peruzzi, Baldaffar
Perzyn, Robert
Pefarefe, Simon
P.Pefne, John
Picart, John
——, Eftienne
——, Bernard
Picinæ, Elizabeth
Piccina, Ifabel, *a Nun*
P.Piccino, Jaques
Piccioni, Matteo
Picquet
Piper, Francis le
Pitau, N.
Podefta, Jo. Andrew
Poilly, Nicolas de
——, Francis de
P.Polemberg, Cornelius
P.Pond
Pontius, Paulus
Pool, Matthew
Popels, John
Poffemieres, Adrian
Preflier, *of* Copen-
    hagen
Procaccini, Camillo
P. Procaccinus, Jul.
    Cæfar.

Q.
Quaft, Peter
Queborn, Crifpin
P.Quiter, Hermannus
    Henry

R.
Randon
Raimondi, Marc.
    Ant.
Ravenna, Silvefter da
Ravennati, Marco
Ravenate, Simon
    Francis
Ravenftein, Gafpar
Regnaffon, N.
P.Rembrandt, van Rhin
Reverdin, *or* Raven-
    ftein
P.Ribera, Giufeppi
Ricci, Jo. Baptift
Ridolfi, P.
Robetta
Rochfort, de
Roger
Roghmans, Giertruy
Rogheman, Hendr.
    Lambert
Roli, Jofeph Maria
Romfteadt, Chrifto-
    pher
P. Rofa, Salvator
Roffi, Hieronymus
——, Henrico
——, Domenico di
P. Rofa, Martino
    Roulet,

Roulet, Jo. Louis
Rouflel, Paul
Rouflelet, Giles
P.Rubens, Sir Peter Paul
Rucholle, P.
P.———, Ægidius
Rugeri, Guido.

S.

Sadeler, Raphael
———, John
———, Rodolph
———, Ægidius
———, Juftus
Saenredam, John
P.Salamanca, Antonio
Salimbeni, Ventura
Salmenicius, Andreas
Sandrart, John Jacob
P.———, Joachim
P.———, Sufanna
Sarrabat, John
Sáraceni, Carlo
Sarragon, John
Sauvé, John
Scalzi, Lodovico
Scaminoffi, Raffaello
Scaramuccia, Luigi
Schauflig, Hans
Schenk, Peter
P.Schon, Martin
Schoonebeek, Adam
Schorel, John
Scotin, G.
———, J. B.
Scorza, Simbaldo

Scuppen
Sebenzanus
Secu, Martin de
Scruuter, P.
Septimius, Hercules
Setti
Scupel, John a
Sezenius, Valentinus
Sichen, Cornelius
Silveftre, Sufanna
———, Ifrael
Simon, Peter
———, John
Simmóneau, Car. *fen.*
———, Car. *jun.*
Sirani, Giovanni
P.———, Elizabetha
P.———, Jo. Andrea
Skenius,Bartholomew
Smeltzing, John
Smidtz, *of* Berlin
Smith, John
P.Smith, Thomas
Snyers, Hendrick
Sole, Virgilius
Sole, Jo. Jofeph da
Sorito, Jo. Baptift
Souberaine
Soutman, Peter
Spagnoletto
Specchi, Aleffandro
Spiez, Hubert
P.Spierre, Franccfco
Spirinx
P.Steen, Francifcus
Stella, Claudius

Ste-

Stephani, P.
Stephanoni, Pietro
P.Stivens, Peter
Stimer, Tobias
Stock, Andreas
Stoltzius
Strada, Vespasiano
Stringa, Francesco
Stuerhelt, F.
Suavius, Lombart
Suruge
Sustermans, Lombart
Suyderhoef, John
Swanenberg, William
Sweerts, Michael
Sylvett, John

T.

Tardieu, Nicolas
Tasiniere, George
Tavernier, M.
P. Tempesta, Domenico
———, Antonio
P. Terzi, Francesco
Testa, Pietro
———, Julio Cesare
Testana, Joseph
———, Jo. Baptist
Thelot, Jo. Philip
Thibout, B.
Thomassin, E.
———, H. S. *jun.*
Thourneissen, H.
P.Tibaldi, Domenico
Tib6

Timus, L.
Tinti, Lorenzo
Tomasini, Filippo
Tompson, Philip
———, Robert
P.Torre, Flaminio
Torrebat, Francois
Trento, Antonio da
Troscel, B.
———, John
Trouvain, A.
Troyen, John.

V.

Vaccario, Andrea
Vænius, Gisbert
Vaillant, William
———, William
Valder, John
Valet, William
P.Valesio, G. Luigi
Valk, John
———, Gerard
Vallée, S.
Valleius, A.
Van Ælst, Nicolas
—— Audenard, R.
—— Boons, David
—— Boucle
—— Bremden, D.
—— Craen
—— Culmhac, Hans
—— Dalen, C. *sen.*
—— Dalen, C. *jun.*
—— Dyck, Sir Anthony
—— Gunst, Philip
Van

Vifker, L.

——, Nicolas

Vivares, F.

P.Vivien, John

Ulric, Henry

Voerierot, Peter

. Voet, Alexander, *jun.*

, Vouillemont, Sel.

Vorft, Robert de

Vos, Martin de

P. Vofterman, Lucas, *fen.*

——————, Lucas, *jun.*

W.

Wagman, Hendrick

Waldreick

Waterlo, Antonius

Watteau

Waumans, Coénrad

Weigel, Chriftopher

White, Robert

Widerman, Élias

Wierx, Anthony

——, Hieronymus

Will, J. G.

Wilant, J. J.

Wingendorf, G.

Wirix, John

Wolfgang, G. A.

P.Wolgemut, Michael

P.Wormache, Antonius

Z.

S. Zabello, Jo. Fran- cefco

Zagel, Mattheus

——, Theodore

Zani, Jo. Baptift

Zarlati, Giofeffo

Zazingeri

Zenoi, Domenico

Zink, Martin

Zylvedt, A.

Zyll, C.

F I N I S.

www.ingramcontent.com/pod-product-compliance
Lightning Source LLC
Chambersburg PA
CBHW020504270326

41926CB00008B/735